THE School
Leadership
Triangle

THE School Leadership Triangle

From Compliance to Innovation

Paul L. Kimmelman
Foreword by M. René Islas

CORWIN
A SAGE Company

For information:

Corwin
A SAGE Company
2455 Teller Road
Thousand Oaks, California 91320
(800) 233-9936
Fax: (800) 417-2466
www.corwin.com

SAGE India Pvt. Ltd.
B 1/I 1 Mohan Cooperative
 Industrial Area
Mathura Road, New Delhi 110 044
India

SAGE Ltd.
1 Oliver's Yard
55 City Road
London EC1Y 1SP
United Kingdom

SAGE Asia-Pacific Pte. Ltd.
33 Pekin Street #02-01
Far East Square
Singapore 048763

Printed in the United States of America

Library of Congress Cataloging-in-Publication Data

Kimmelman, Paul L.
The school leadership triangle: from compliance to innovation/Paul L. Kimmelman.
    p. cm.
Includes bibliographical references and index.
ISBN 978-1-4129-7804-0 (pbk.)

    1. Educational leadership—United States. 2. School management and organization—United States. I. Title.

LB2805.K51655 2010
371.2—dc22

2009048072

This book is printed on acid-free paper.

10 11 12 13 14 10 9 8 7 6 5 4 3 2 1

Acquisitions Editor:	Dan Alpert
Associate Editor:	Megan Bedell
Production Editor:	Cassandra Margaret Seibel
Copy Editor:	Sarah J. Duffy
Typesetter:	C&M Digitals (P) Ltd.
Proofreader:	Christina West
Indexer:	Terri Corry
Cover Designer:	Rose Storey

Contents

Foreword

The education profession occupies a well-deserved position of honor in the hearts and minds of Americans. Most Americans fondly recall the "life-changing" impact that one teacher had on their lives. Many remember the teacher, or teachers, who inspired them and put them on the course to becoming the citizens they are today. Our nation's leaders and public figures also respect the role of educators in society. In the final debate prior to the 2008 presidential election, both candidates, John McCain and Barack Obama, spent significant time discussing the need for greater rewards for effective teachers. Most notably, public opinion polls show that Americans revere teachers, with the teaching profession repeatedly topping the list on surveys identifying the most prestigious occupations (Harris Interactive, 2007). All of this confirms that the public overwhelmingly admires the education profession.

Does this admiration carry over to the education profession's leaders? Well, there is a disturbing trend. According to a study by Rosenthal, Pittinsky, Purvin, and Montoya (2007), from the John F. Kennedy School of Government's Center for Public Leadership at Harvard University, the public's confidence in the education sector's leadership has eroded for two consecutive years. A saving grace for educational leaders is that they are not singled out. According to the study, "more than three quarters of those surveyed now believe there is a leadership crisis in this country, up from 69% in 2006 and 65% in 2005" (p. 1).

The decline in the public's faith in today's educational leaders has serious implications for the profession and, more important, children in our nation's schools. Already, we are seeing the manifestation of this declining confidence. More parents are looking for, and choosing, alternatives to traditional educational settings for their children. According to the Center for Education Reform, over 1.2 million students were educated in 4,100 charter schools around the nation during the 2007–2008 school year. This represents a one-year growth of 8% in the number of new charter schools. Data show that home schooling is on the rise, and a majority of parents cite dissatisfaction with academic instruction as the main reason. Despite these shifts, a promising factor for educators is that the public still believes that professional educators should be making decisions about schools. Overwhelmingly, they report that educators, not businesspeople or politicians, should guide decisions about our nation's schools.

It is for these reasons that this book by Paul Kimmelman on the pressing issues of compliance, leadership, and innovation in education is so timely and important for the field. Paul asks readers to consider the opportunity to leverage policy and compliance structures in order to make the changes they know will benefit children. He helps draw inferences from the study of leadership theory, about which many of us could use a refresher. Finally, he makes the important call for innovation in education. Paul's three points sound the alarm for what is now critically needed in education to protect its important status in our country and restore faith that educators and the education system will prepare the nation's youth to lead our now global society.

The public desperately wants to support educators, and I believe reflection on Paul's clear insights and historical perspectives in this book will help the field protect its revered position in society. I offer the following three points of advice to those who will become the new leaders in education, which correlate with Paul's themes of compliance, leadership, and innovation.

EMBRACE AND LEVERAGE LEGAL/POLICY FRAMEWORKS AND COMPLIANCE STRUCTURES

Educators have a tradition of being extremely obedient. They are responsive to laws governing their practice and often follow mandates without complaint. This does not mean that they agree with all of the policy mandates to which they are subjected. In fact, they are usually the first to see the flaws in education laws and regulations that govern schools. However, out of respect and deference to policymakers, they dutifully execute. Despite this compliance, policymakers and the general public often feel dissatisfied with the response of educators. The critical question is, Why the dissatisfaction? Obviously, there is a mismatch between public and policymaker expectations and educator actions.

I propose that educators will thrive and public leaders will increase their faith in them when educators work to understand the underlying motivations for the laws, policies, and regulations imposed on them. So I suggest that the job of new leaders in education is to help educators discover the authentic motivations behind legal and policy frameworks and work to address those while they comply with the bureaucratic rules. I am confident that when this occurs, the public will increase its satisfaction with schools and educators will feel fulfilled by their work.

INCREASE ATTENTION
AND SENSITIVITY TO THE NEEDS
AND DESIRES OF EXTERNAL INFLUENCERS

Understanding and embracing policy actions is one responsive step that educators can take to protect their status in society and improve teaching and learning in schools. A more proactive step that new leaders in education ought to take is to become more externally focused. As the world we live in grows more interconnected, we must remind ourselves that leadership occurs within a social context. Throughout history, schools have enjoyed some protection from external pressures. Professional educators maintained control over their own domain and were, for the most part, free from micromanagement from political and business leaders. The general public practiced deference to teacher authority and professional judgment. That is all in the past. In the current age of interconnectedness, fueled by Web 2.0 technologies such as blogs, podcasts, and wikis, the schoolhouse doors have blown wide open.

The world today requires leaders to be more perceptive than in the past. Leaders in education can regain their status as "thought leaders," like past luminaries John Dewey and Albert Shanker, if they carefully observe the world around them while attending to the core work of educating students within the schoolhouse walls. Leaders in education should expose themselves to new thinking outside of the traditional education community. They must regularly scout out what's on the minds of parents, business leaders, and national leaders inside and outside the education arena. This proactive stance will allow them to be active in constructing solutions and contributing to policy debates rather than merely reacting to them.

SUPPORT FOCUSED INNOVATION
IN SCHOOLS AND CLASSROOMS

The final recommendation for new leaders in education is to create an environment that fosters innovation in schools and classrooms. It is no secret that schools have been fairly resistant to change. Many people argue that the majority of classrooms are no different today than they were a century ago despite the completely different world that currently exists. Critics say that education systems retain outdated models of learning that no longer fit with students today nor prepare students for future societal needs.

This can and must change. New leaders should establish a culture of innovation in schools. They can foster this culture by creating processes such as structured and facilitated collaboration. It is in these processes that educators will be empowered to identify barriers to success, for students as well as themselves, and develop effective solutions. I am confident that this empowerment will engender a feeling of self-efficacy that will promote retention of educators as well as motivate new promising individuals to join the profession.

CLOSING THOUGHTS

As you read this book, I encourage you to accept Paul's challenge to move away from outmoded educational leadership and join the ranks of new leaders in education. I believe that your contribution in embracing compliance, assuming leadership, and fostering innovation will ensure that education retains its critical role in making America great.

M. René Islas
Vice President
B&D Consulting

Preface

Federal Policy/Compliance, Leadership and Innovation

A Triangulation for School Improvement Initiatives

T his book is intended for educators to address three important questions that don't often get much attention as part of a comprehensive plan for reflecting on their systemic improvement work.

WHAT WERE THEY THINKING?

Congress passes federal laws such as the No Child Left Behind (NCLB) Act that require compliance, but it is rare for practitioners, those who must implement the law, to create an opportunity to understand exactly what the members of Congress were thinking when they passed the laws. What is the history of the calls for education reform, and how did they lead to Congress finally passing the most intrusive, sanctions-laden law for states and school districts ever under the auspices of the Elementary and Secondary Education Act? More important, how can compliance-driven laws be used to create a sense of urgency for their intended goals yet be flexible enough to appropriately be a driver for the needed change?

Educators often believe that their counterparts in the business world don't have to undergo the same scrutiny that NCLB has placed on them. To help dispel that misconception, this book includes a brief discussion and personal comments from former Congressman Mike Oxley, one of the coauthors of the Sarbanes-Oxley Act, a significant ethics law passed by

Congress that relates to business and financial reporting. Comments from other members of Congress and educators regarding NCLB compliance, leadership, and innovation are also included.

Fortunately, this book has taken me longer to write than originally intended. For that reason, newer events enabled me to reflect more precisely on what I was hoping to accomplish by writing the book. Clearly, the financial events at the end of 2008 parallel some of the issues that arose with NCLB. While Sarbanes-Oxley was intended to bring about more ethical behavior on the part of CEOs and their companies and accuracy in financial reporting, the financial crisis of 2008 demonstrated that the law wasn't entirely successful. And to help some of those companies, it didn't take Congress long to find nearly a trillion—yes that is *trillion* with a T—dollars to attempt to fix the problem. Yet educators who had been plodding along with NCLB, a law that imposed strict and punitive sanctions for not making required improvement, were not getting even the benefit of funding at the authorized levels. I am not suggesting that money is the only answer to fixing organizational problems. But when CEOs of major U.S. companies failed, their companies weren't reconstituted, nor were their employees replaced as the result of failing to meet a federal compliance requirement. But be careful what you ask for! By February 2009, Congress passed the American Recovery and Reinvestment Act, better known as the stimulus bill, and put approximately one hundred billion dollars in the K–12 funding pipeline, nearly doubling the U.S. Department of Education budget. Granted, the money is a one-time infusion for education. But it is unprecedented and, at the outset, not laden with overly burdensome compliance regulations, and it includes funds for innovation. Do you think policymakers won't be looking for improved performance of U.S. students? And if the results aren't obvious, the argument for increased education funding could be somewhat shallow in the future.

I believe in the fundamental principles of compliance-driven legislation. Without some sanctions, it is difficult to get people motivated to embrace change. Educators were slow to address some of the critically important provisions of NCLB, such as teacher quality, proficiency achievement for all students, and using research and knowledge to make decisions about programs for their schools. Compliance with NCLB changed all that. But it remains open to dispute how so much money was found so quickly to address a business "crisis" yet the education "crisis," often cited as critical to the successful future of the United States and its ability to compete in the global marketplace, couldn't muster the type of support it needed in Congress to see if money really could make a difference. We will soon find out. Hopefully this stimulus money will change the culture of schools to allow for less bureaucracy in decision making and more emphasis on organizing teams to engage in innovation and creating new products, programs, and practices that work.

WHERE ARE WE GOING AND WHERE HAVE WE BEEN?

Education has traditionally operated from the premise of the "great man theory," that is, the superintendent and principal are the formal leaders. Yet more and more literature is being written about teachers as leaders and distributive leadership, concepts that empower others in schools, such as teachers, to make important decisions regarding school issues. But how can teachers be expected to function effectively as leaders if they don't have appropriate background on the research and evolution of leadership theory? All effective leaders need to have a context for their leadership work. What is the contemporary thinking about how leaders function using a process that aligns with followers?

WHAT, NO SILVER BULLET?

The 21st century is about innovation in a global, flat, digital, information-laden, and knowledge-based world economy. Yet what passes as innovation in education isn't normally transformational or related to "breakthrough" and doesn't always result in real improvement. Additionally, really successful innovative educational practices rarely become known to all educators who could benefit from using them. This is because there is no effective dissemination process that transcends every district and school in the United States to communicate innovative products, programs, and practices. What is interesting to note is that even sports fans are using innovative thinking and technology to create a national network to connect them and distribute information about their teams. They are creating SportsBlog Nation, and it is intended to cover almost all sports, leagues, teams, and players (Hart, 2009).

Just think about this. Medicine has produced some incredible innovations that transformed the profession in profound ways with amazing results for patients. The laser transformed modern corrective vision surgery, and scalpels are now a tool of the past. The laser for correcting vision has made eye surgery faster, safer, less expensive, less intrusive, and more effective and has reduced recovery time. In orthopedic surgery, Dr. Bryan Neal, my wife's doctor who treated her when she broke her wrist, said that hip and knee replacement have transformed the lives of those who have had these procedures. Without the innovation of that type of surgery, including the replacement parts, patients would be required to live their lives with considerable pain.

Where are the parallels in education? Educators are still looking for the innovative silver bullet that will solve some of the most challenging problems related to accountability compliance requirements. It won't come unless they understand what innovation is and how it can be implemented effectively in a school setting. And innovation may not come cheaply. It may necessitate incentive funding to really produce the learning equivalent of laser surgery and hip/knee replacement. One can only hope that the funds in the American Recovery and Reinvestment Act that are specifically targeted for innovation will produce some innovative ideas that will dramatically result in improved products, programs, practices, and learning in America's schools. The key, however, is to provide the appropriate setting in those schools to spawn innovative thinking. These funds might just do that!

Acknowledgments

Writing a book is not merely an author-driven experience. It takes a lot of support and cooperation from many people. I want to express my sincere appreciation to the following people and be very clear that without their help, support, and advice, I would not have been able to write this book.

First, I want to convey my deep appreciation to my wife, Marsha. Not only was she helpful with her ideas and editing, but she has a way of "pushing" me to finish work that I am reluctant to do. She has always been a motivation for me to succeed.

My children, Leah and Renee, and my son-in-law, Scott, are always supportive and help me reflect on my thinking. Leah is a successful school principal; Renee and Scott are successful corporate executives. I am also fortunate that my brother, Jim, and his wife, Sandy, were willing to offer critiques of my work. Jim, a periodontist, asked many questions throughout the writing of this book from the perspective of someone who isn't a practicing K–12 educator.

I owe the theme of this book and the inspiration for writing it to Learning Point Associates CEO Gina Burkhardt. Not only is Gina visionary in her thinking, but her insistence on quality and her candid comments are important to me in my work.

I could not write or do my work without the great colleagues I have at Learning Point Associates. They are a deeply passionate group committed to helping improve public education. They fully understand the challenges facing states and school districts in a standards-based, accountability-driven education environment. I extend a very special thank you to Matt Burke of our Regional Educational Laboratory Midwest for designing the National Assessment of Education Progress graphic in Chapter 1.

I was fortunate to have a very supportive and equally excellent editor at Corwin. Dan Alpert was available to share his thinking on my writing and offer critically important advice and suggestions. He also has a way of understanding me, which isn't always a simple task.

René Islas authored an excellent Foreword for this book. René has been a friend of mine for a long time and is deeply committed to public education.

A special thank you to Sir Michael Barber for writing about his important study on world-class schools in a brief essay for this book, which appears at the end of Chapter 1. Sir Michael and I have been friends for many years, and he gave me one of my most memorable moments when we visited 10 Downing Street and met with Prime Minister Tony Blair's policy advisor.

And I would be remiss if I did not publicly acknowledge the members of Congress who willingly (well, almost willingly) gave me their valuable time to discuss their opinions on my topics. I offer my deep appreciation to Representatives Biggert, Boehner, Castle, DeLauro, Holt, Kirk, Manzullo, McKeon, Miller, and Sarbanes, Senator Gregg, former Speaker of the House Hastert, and former Representative Oxley.

I also want to acknowledge the staff in the congressional offices. They work with little recognition, yet they persevere over long hours, engaging in significant policy debates about how the federal government should be involved in education. They get far less credit for their knowledge and work than they deserve.

Also I extend my deep appreciation to many other people who took time to be interviewed by me. Their thoughts as experts on education were critically important to me being able to offer diverse perspectives on compliance, leadership, and innovation. Thanks to Debra Brydon, from CyberText in Australia; former Florida Governor Jeb Bush; Dan Domenech, from the American Association of School Administrators; Jeffrey Elliott, from Advanced Academics; Jennifer Fisler, from Messiah College; Bob Hughes, from the National Institute of School Leadership; Gary Huggins, from the Aspen NCLB Commission; Jim Kohlmoos, from Knowledge Alliance; Paul Leather, from the New Hampshire State Department of Education; Chuck Morris, from the San Diego Unified School District; Dr. George "Pinky" Nelson, former Shuttle Astronaut and now at Western Washington University; John Pipino, from Doblin; Neale Pitches, from Pacific Learning; Kathy Reynolds, from the Washoe County (Nevada) School District; former U.S. Secretary of Education Richard Riley; Andy Scantland, from Advanced Academics; Sandy Speicher, from IDEO; and Tim Waters, from Mid-continent Research for Education and Learning.

Finally, this book concludes with some brief comments from Learning Point Associates CEO Gina Burkhardt. It was her thinking about compliance, leadership, and innovation that was the inspiration for me to work on this challenging project. There would be no better way to conclude this book than to read her final comments.

PUBLISHER'S ACKNOWLEDGMENTS

Corwin gratefully acknowledges the contributions of the following reviewers:

Kenneth Arndt, Superintendent
Community Unit School District #300, Carpentersville, IL

Carol S. Cash, Assistant Professor
Virginia Tech, Blacksburg, VA

Douglas Gordon Hesbol, Superintendent of Schools
Laraway Community Consolidated School District 70C, Joliet, IL

Dan Lawson, Superintendent of Schools
Tullahoma City Schools, Tullahoma, TN

Kevin S. Peart, Assistant Superintendent
Lampeter-Strasburg School District, Lampeter, PA

About the Author

Paul L. Kimmelman is senior adviser to the CEO at Learning Point Associates. He has served as a consultant to the Qualifications and Curriculum Authority in England, and senior consultant to Project 2061 Professional Development Programs of the American Association for the Advancement of Science. He worked in K–12 education for more than 30 years as a teacher, high school assistant principal, middle school principal, assistant superintendent, and superintendent, and he has been an adjunct professor at several colleges and universities. Currently, he is adjunct professor at Argosy University. As superintendent in Lima, Ohio, he worked to help the district successfully comply with a federal desegregation order. He served as president of the First in the World Consortium when he was a superintendent in Illinois. The consortium was a collaborative group of school districts that were the first noncountry group to participate in the Third International Mathematics and Science Study. He has authored numerous articles and publications on education and presented at national and state education meetings. He is author of *Implementing NCLB: Creating a Knowledge Framework to Support School Improvement* (2006) and coauthor (with David Kroeze) of *Achieving World-Class Schools: Mastering School Improvement Using a Genetic Model* (2002). He was appointed by former U.S. Secretary of Education Richard Riley to the National Commission on Mathematics and Science Teaching, chaired by former senator and astronaut John Glenn, and served on the Third International Mathematics and Science Study Technical Review Panel. He was also appointed by U.S. Secretary of Education Rod Paige to serve on the Teacher Assistance Corps and participated in the Teacher-to-Teacher project, offering sessions on building teacher leaders.

Introduction

The future of education will be less about compliance, more about schools that have the capacity to achieve successful learning outcomes for their students using proven delivery models; education will be designed to meet the needs of schools' constituents rather than those who work in them. That comment is made by many who are predicting a different future for U.S. education. Even if it is true, federal laws will still require compliance and education leaders will have to utilize a variety of effective leadership strategies coupled with innovation to be successful enough in a rapidly changing, globally competitive world in order to offer that constituent-based education.

I have been involved in education for more than 40 years. Approximately 34 of those years were spent working in K–12 education. Most of that experience was as a school administrator, including 1 year as a high school assistant principal, 6 years as a middle school principal, 6 years as an assistant superintendent, and 16 years as a superintendent. Presently, I work as a senior advisor in an education consulting and research firm, with the primary responsibility of overseeing congressional relations and federal education policy. In addition, I served as program coordinator for organizational leadership for 2 years in the College of Psychology and Behavioral Sciences at the for-profit Argosy University in Schaumburg, Illinois. My lens for viewing education enables me to observe both traditional and nontraditional approaches to 21st-century education delivery strategies. My purpose in writing this book is to offer a framework for important discussion regarding the process of school improvement. It is not to tell readers what to do. Educators hear far too often, "Do this, or do that." Rather, my goal is to encourage professional study groups to engage in thinking about how they can improve their organizations while reflecting on compliance, leadership, and innovation. It is my belief that much of the knowledge needed to successfully improve schools resides in the current workforce, and it is the process of implementation that needs refining. Underpinning that process is the ability to carefully reflect on what you are attempting to do and asking the right questions. School improvement teams could be more effective if they spent more time thinking about the right questions rather that merely starting by analyzing solutions.

I offer a brief explanation of my career experiences in education not to massage my ego, but rather to offer some credibility for what I present in this book. I have been involved with federal policy as a high school teacher and president of a fairly large and influential teachers' union, as a school superintendent, and as an advisor in an education research and consulting organization working on federal policy. My experience with federal policy dates back to the Nixon administration, when a federal wage price freeze unfairly affected teachers simply because of a law's implementation date. I had just completed a difficult collective bargaining agreement on behalf of our teachers, and the wage price freeze would have imposed an unfair burden on them by not allowing their salary increases to become effective when they returned to work in September. That problem was ultimately corrected with the support of two influential Ohio congressmen and my visit to Washington to meet with staff at the Office of Emergency Preparedness. It was the process of working with congressional leaders and explaining the unfair application of the new federal law to the Office of Emergency Preparedness staff that resulted in modification of some of the provisions that unfairly affected teachers. It was through this experience that I learned an important lesson that has served as a guiding light throughout my career: while you may have to comply with federal laws, you can lead and work diligently to get them modified if you have a rationale that makes sense. I have also had the privilege of testifying before Congress on some issues and offering thoughts about why compliance requirements should be changed.

As a superintendent, I was the president of a consortium of school districts that participated collaboratively in a project on international assessment in mathematics and science. That project was not only innovative, but resulted in President Clinton spending a half day in our district delivering an important education speech to over 5,000 people, the first speech after his second inauguration. That consortium committed to achieving the national goal to make the United States first in the world in mathematics and science by 2000. Beyond just being an innovative concept for local school districts focusing on a national policy goal, the student achievement results of the consortium were equal or nearly equal to the best-achieving countries in the world.

And that is what the First in the World did. There is no better model for what we were trying to do in the entire United States of America than what you have done here. And you should be very proud of yourselves. **(Clinton, 1997)**

My current job has afforded me the opportunity to meet and work with members of Congress and their staffs. Congressional staff have always impressed me with their commitment to and knowledge of the federal policies they are working on and their recognition of the potential implications for practitioners. Their work results in serious compliance efforts for state and local education officials. While the laws aren't always perfect, understanding the context and the thinking of Congress when they were passed is an important aspect of complying with the laws. The staff don't get much attention, but their work has a significant influence on the daily responsibilities of most educators.

The experiences I have mentioned, among many others, have led me to conclude how much compliance with federal policy can impact education leadership and innovation. Figure 0.1 offers a conceptual model of the three key ideas discussed in this book: compliance, leadership and innovation. The notion is that educators operate mostly in the context of a compliance environment. Despite the fact that there is no mention of education in the U.S. Constitution, since NCLB was signed into law in 2002, the role of the federal government has gradually and consistently grown in the operation of state and local school districts. And there is no evidence almost one year into the Obama administration that the federal government's role with respect to compliance will decrease. In fact, there is some indication that it will increase and even impose more daunting challenges for states and local school districts. Thus, compliance will continue to be an important driver of school reform initiatives.

Figure 0.1

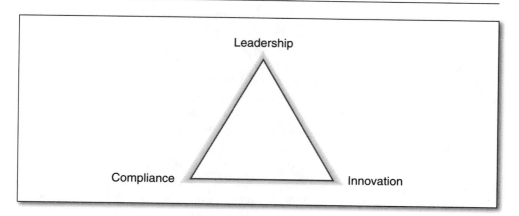

In a compliance environment, it will be absolutely essential for successful school improvement initiatives to have effective leaders and a different leadership model than in the past. Education leadership is undergoing a transformation at the system and building levels. Leaders are emerging from different pathways and training programs. And it is becoming more important for education to embrace new thinking about the role of teachers in the school leadership model by giving them the authority, responsibility, and training to lead improvement initiatives.

Finally, school improvement initiatives will need to be innovative. There is a critically important need for bold, new thinking to achieve successful results in overcoming the most challenging problems confronting educators. Some of those challenges have persisted for decades and are not going to be solved by solutions that have been tried and proven unsuccessful.

Many educators believe that federal policies such as NCLB unfairly mandate federal compliance on their work while others, such as leaders in the business sector, don't have to comply with overly burdensome federal intrusion in their work. I will draw a brief comparison between NCLB and the Sarbanes-Oxley Act (SOX) to exemplify that point. SOX actually did result in significant changes for corporate accountability that mirror many of the concerns educators raised about NCLB and federal involvement. I draw this comparison for two reasons. First, both acts were passed at approximately the same time. Second, both have resulted in similar complaints from leaders in both education and business. I find that ironic. SOX clearly refutes the claim of educators that the federal government doesn't intrude on business with costly, burdensome compliance mandates.

Interestingly, the financial events of 2008 provided a very different scenario for dealing with the consequences of the laws for those expected to comply with them. Some schools were being reconstituted, and some deservedly so, while some businesses were being refinanced with federal dollars despite failing both ethically and practically. One wonders how a for-profit company in a free enterprise system can be more deserving of scarce federal dollars to survive than schools, which were simply closed for not being successful. This is indeed a conundrum.

SOX was the result of years of corporate corruption and misrepresentation of critical financial data and information by those who had a personal stake in their companies. Enron would turn out to be the leading poster child for the law (McLean & Elkind, 2003), although there are others, such as WorldCom and Tyco. Later, U.S. banks, insurance companies, and two of America's large auto manufacturers joined the federal dollar handout line. SOX became law because of corporate leaders being disingenuous with their employees and stockholders and demonstrating that they didn't need to be accountable to them. Despite Congress passing a strict compliance law aimed at businesses, some still did not comply. And many even went on to receive federal support as a result of failing to comply.

NCLB was the result of many years of federally funded programs that produced disappointing achievement outcomes for the students who were supposed to do much better in school as a result of the federal investment in programs to help them. Despite many commissions and reports calling for reforms (Kimmelman, 2006), members of Congress didn't observe the student achievement improvement they felt was necessary in the United States when compared to students in other countries. Thus, Congress passed the most intrusive, sanction-filled federal education law ever after many years of disappointing achievement results for U.S. students and the harsh reality of the need for change. For better or worse, NCLB captured educator attention and has resulted in some meaningful reform efforts. It clearly created a sense of urgency and has led to some positive school reform initiatives such as charter schools, implementation of creative compensation plans for teachers, improved teacher preparation programs, better use of relevant data, and recognition of the specific needs of students who have not met achievement goals.

As we have seen, NCLB and SOX resulted in similar outcries from both education and business leaders. Despite overall low achievement in education for students in federal programs and the incredibly disingenuous information and corrupt practices in business, neither group of leaders was willing to accept federal intervention, arguing that it had no place in their workplaces. They argued that Congress was being overly intrusive, there was no basis for the laws, they were unfunded mandates, and they were overly prescriptive. The irony is in the alignment of the complaints and their similarity. The contextual basis for the laws was not the primary discussion; rather, the focus was on whether the federal government was being overly intrusive in areas where it had little or no legal authority to legislate. One member of Congress I interviewed strongly supports that notion.

In order to gain a better understanding of these laws, I interviewed some members of Congress for this book to understand their perspectives on the laws, the reasons why they supported or opposed them, and their thoughts about leadership and innovation. These elected officials all had substantive comments, and the purpose of the interviews was to give readers a firsthand account of their thinking. It was not to criticize them or to argue whether they were right or wrong. Members of Congress are elected and therefore are entitled to vote what they believe is in the best interests of the people they represent. My aim was to demonstrate that federal policy plays a significant role in leadership because of the need for compliance and that leaders, whether they are in education or business, must be more cognizant of what happens in Congress.

I also interviewed a host of other people in various fields. Debra Brydon discussed her innovative approach to offering an administrative conference in the Northern Territory in Australia. Former Florida Governor Jeb Bush provided insight on the need for education reform from the perspective of a state policy leader who actually led education reform at the state level. Dan Domenech, with the American Association of School Administrators, offered his thinking on school leadership based on his years of school administration, as superintendent of Fairfax County (Virginia) Schools, and in the private sector with McGraw-Hill. Jeffrey Elliott and Andy Scantland, from Advanced Academics, have been involved in delivering online education and partnering with public schools and states. They provided some valuable suggestions for the future implementation of online education. Jennifer Fisler, at Messiah College, is promoting the importance of teacher leadership in her role as a department chairman and assistant professor in a program for preservice teachers. Gary Huggins, from the Aspen Institute NCLB Commission, had keen insight to offer on NCLB after participating in hearings across the United States and listening to people talk about what improvements are needed when the law is reauthorized. Bob Hughes, from the National Institute for School Leadership, has a diverse background in leadership, and his organization is offering new ideas on leadership training for school leaders. Jim Kohlmoos, from Knowledge Alliance, has been pursuing his vision for a federal law supporting knowledge and innovation in education and creating an office in the U.S. Department of Education to implement it. Paul Leather, from the New Hampshire State Department of Education, has been working on an innovative program in to improve high school education in his state. Chuck Morris is a veteran school administrator currently serving as deputy superintendent of the San Diego (California) Unified School District. Dr. George "Pinky" Nelson, former shuttle astronaut, now oversees mathematics and science teacher education at Western Washington University. He has had success with his teacher preparation program and improving student achievement in mathematics and science. He also served as executive director of Project 2061 at the American Association for the Advancement of Science and has devoted his postastronaut career to improving education. John Pipino offered insight on innovation from his highly regarded company, Doblin. Neale Pitches, from Pacific Learning, has devoted many years to offering high-quality literacy products and helping all schools have the opportunity to use them regardless of their technology platforms. Former U.S. Secretary of Education Richard Riley was recognized by many for his outstanding leadership in education. Since leaving the department, he has continued to promote high-quality education for all students. Sandy Speicher, from the highly regarded design thinking company IDEO, offered some valuable insight on how to innovate. Finally, Tim Waters, from Mid-continent Research for Education and Learning, regarded as one of the leading experts on the topic, offered an outstanding review of leadership in education. Kathy Reynolds, of the Washoe County (Nevada) School District, is using the Advanced Academics program in her district and offered insight into using online education as part of the public school curriculum.

The Foreword for this book was written by René Islas, who is currently vice president at B&D Consulting. René has a considerable background in education policy, not the least of which was his experience at the U.S. Department of Education as chief of staff to the assistant secretary of education and his work on implementing NCLB.

Sir Michael Barber, now with McKinsey Consulting, is a former advisor to British Prime Minister Tony Blair. He is recognized by many as one of the most knowledgeable school reform thinkers in the world, and he contributed a short essay on world-class schools to this book.

Gina Burkhardt, CEO of Learning Point Associates, concludes the book with her final comments on compliance, leadership, and innovation. Gina understands and has accomplished real organizational transformation at LPA.

CHAPTER 1

In Chapter 1, I briefly discuss the history of some key education reform proposals over the last half century and the personal thoughts of members of Congress who were involved in the original NCLB and SOX legislation. I address the notion that federal policy plays a critical role in the daily work of leaders, regardless of whether they are in education or business, because of their need to comply with it. Compliance requires effective leadership, and to be effective in leading organizations in a globally competitive environment, it is important, if not essential, to encourage innovation as part of improvement initiatives.

Compliance with NCLB has resulted in achievement and teaching improvements in education, but not necessarily real systemic organizational growth. Most compliance efforts have been incremental, much like the continuous improvement thinking of the 1990s. For example, in NCLB there are many variables that make the adequate yearly progress goal (every student in Grades 3–8 achieving proficiency on state tests in reading and mathematics by 2014) of 100% success laudable. But the reality is that achievement of that goal is more than likely unattainable. SOX can require honest financial reporting, but if there isn't a systemic culture of integrity to comply with the law, it doesn't prevent fraud. Federal policy can be a driver of change, but compliance alone is unlikely to produce long-term systemic results that build a better system. Federal policy is an important ingredient in the process, but it can't be a stand-alone component. It is merely that driver of change. Real systemic change comes from effective leadership and innovation.

Both NCLB and SOX place a great deal of responsibility on leaders in education and business. In the 1990s, the continuous improvement efforts in business and education did not achieve their intended results:

> That failure was attributed to the silver bullet syndrome, aka, magic pills for business ills. It was a reactionary stance that focused on compliance and correction and was not the ideal way to do something. They failed to build a necessary critical mass. When the low-hanging fruit was picked clean, and the painstaking work of instilling a true system-wide routine for finding and solving tougher problems began, they went searching for a new bullet. (May, 2007, p. 41)

Calls for reform that go unheeded can result in federal intervention. Congress tends to react to public outcries and is not usually a proactive legislative body. NCLB was the result of years of reports calling for systemic improvements that were basically ignored, which allowed many students who needed a better education to fall further and further behind. SOX was the result of egregious corporate behavior and greed. In both instances, Congress passed what it thought were laws that responded to the public insistence for change and imposed rigorous compliance requirements on both education and business leaders.

CHAPTER 2

In Chapter 2, I briefly review the history of leadership theories and current thinking about what is needed for effective leadership. There are some questions that need to be explored: What leadership context is needed in order to comply with a federal policy and to improve an education organization? How does innovation fit in the leadership plan? After more than one hundred years of leadership research, there is no conclusive definition of one best leadership practice, trait, or behavior. But that doesn't mean it is not important for those who want to lead to have a basic understanding of the leadership theories and be able to apply different strategies in order to meet the needs of the various situations leaders confront on a daily basis. The plethora of theories provides a leadership toolbox that can be applied effectively to meet the needs of a specific situation.

Most everyone has an idea about what effective leadership is. These ideas generally focus on the leader, but it may be more important to focus on the followers and the context of the situation where leadership is needed. Leadership theories continue to evolve, and it is highly unlikely that one person, strategy, practice, or trait will work all the time. It is more critical to have a broad understanding of leadership and know how and when to apply various practices in order to be successful. Schools are realistic examples of how important it is for leaders to respond to highly diverse groups of stakeholders and rapidly changing situations.

There is clearly a movement in education for more accountability from leaders and an emphasis on outcomes rather than inputs.

> I think in several key areas of society in general, breaking out of measuring inputs and instead measuring outputs is critical. You would hope that those of us in Congress could decide what success is. We ought to have a full and complete debate as to what success is in objective measurements. **(Congressman Mark Kirk, personal communication, July 25, 2007)**

Thus, leaders need to be cognizant not only of their leadership strategies, but also of how using knowledge, research, and data play a role in that process. In 2002, Congress reauthorized the Education Sciences Reform Act, which provides for improvement of federal education research, statistics, evaluation, information, and dissemination. It created the Institute for Education Sciences, which calls for the gold standard of research by replicating in education what transpires in medicine. Medical research provides a solid model for education researchers, but it is not without its weaknesses. Educators might be well served by such high-quality research, but it isn't the one and only solution to solving the myriad of problems associated with educating highly diverse student populations. Effective leaders need to use innovative solutions that work in this new global era.

Chapter 2 reviews a number of leadership theories and thoughts about how contemporary ideas about leadership can fit into the school setting. It also provides examples for school leaders to consider when reflecting on their own situations.

CHAPTER 3

Chapter 3 is about innovation and why this is an important topic for educators. In general, educators tend to move from one initiative or fad to another without building a solid knowledge base and making incremental improvements until there is flawless implementation of the initiative. Many of the great innovations are the result of continuously making small improvements to something that already existed. Unfortunately, innovation has not been a high priority for educators, and few, if any, transformational innovations in education have produced undeniable success regardless of who was teaching or what was being taught.

Innovation doesn't have to be a highly complex technological device that wows consumers. In education, innovation needs to be something that makes a challenging task much easier on a daily basis and results in success. In some presentations I have given, I have often used the metaphor of a paper clip as a great innovation. The paper clip is over one hundred years old, yet it remains an important part of everyday work and makes the task of organizing and holding multiple sheets of paper together much easier. It isn't overly complex, yet is truly an amazing innovation. The laser for corrective eye surgery transformed the surgical process. And although far more complex than a paper clip, its success has been an important innovation for medicine. Educators must find innovative ideas that will lead to greater teaching and learning success in a globally competitive world. Doing things the same way will only lead to similar results.

Toyota has been a leader in business innovation. Pacific Learning released literacy curriculum materials that are integrated with the use of an interactive whiteboard. I discuss what Toyota and Pacific Learning and others have done with the hope that their ideas can be transferred to school innovation initiatives.

CHAPTER 4

Chapter 4 is a summary of my final thoughts and conclusions on compliance, leadership, and innovation. From the words of my CEO, Gina Burkhardt, who introduced the importance of linking these three topics, I have attempted to articulate a realistic approach to how they can be implemented in a 21st-century education environment. A brief essay of summary comments is provided by Gina at the end of Chapter 4.

SUMMARY

This book is an attempt to triangulate compliance, leadership, and innovation. Using these three important but somewhat disconnected concepts, I hope to offer a framework for their use and for those who want to lead improvement initiatives in a compliance-driven environment. This is not a long book filled with pages upon pages of information. Instead, it is a thin book filled with ideas that I hope will be used in professional study groups as the first step in the process of working on school improvement initiatives. I don't offer a book of recipes, but rather the context for getting started. Leadership is a critically important component of school improvement, but it is often overlooked. I hope this book will encourage education leaders to think with a compliance, leadership, and innovation mindset. Mental models, those pictures in the minds of leaders about how things should look, are known to be helpful when working on complex problems. This book should be the foundation for teams to discuss the key issues in order to make substantive improvements in their organizations while addressing the challenges of complying with federal laws and other regulation-driven requirements. The concepts are based on three critical ideas for leading schools or other organizations to a point at which they will be conceptually prepared to meet the needs of the next generation of students and workers. While most adults currently working in the education infrastructure have been trained in traditional delivery models of instruction, today's students are digital natives. They form their own online social communities using sites such as Facebook, they communicate digitally using cell phones and text messaging, they maintain their music and pictures digitally and even take online courses offered through accredited schools. All of this can be done without ever having to leave the confines of their homes. These evolving trends will be critical to complying, leading, and innovating in schools and workplaces that meet the needs of their stakeholders.

The traditional concept of education is that you have to go to a brick-and-mortar school, be taught by a teacher who is physically in the class-room, and socialize through groups sponsored by the school and the community. These schools are led by a principal operating in a traditional bureaucratic hierarchy. The theories of effective education leaders are supported by research that focuses on the behaviors of leaders despite more contemporary research suggesting that leadership is dependent on the followers and the contextual situation rather than just the behavior of the leader (Bennis, 2007). And schools are struggling with costly mandates that require specific achievement goals using an industrial model rather than being offered incentives to try innovative ideas that might address the myriad of diverse learners throughout their halls.

If any profession has been devoid of innovation, it is education. When one looks for the education product, program, or practice that unquestionably produces high-quality results, makes the task less complex, and was a result of innovation, the view is pretty dim. Unlike in medicine, where corrective vision surgery has been almost completely transformed through the use of the laser, education is still searching for something that will empower teachers to achieve success beyond their greatest belief. As Thomas Friedman (2005) made clear in his now famous book, *The World Is Flat*, without innovation in U.S. education, the nation's ability to successfully train and educate its students so that they can function in a new world will be seriously jeopardized. Notice I didn't use the business mantra of "compete or train for the workforce." In many respects, the business community has leveraged its bets on American education. Some of the companies complaining about the number of education problems in U.S. schools are multinational and use a global workforce regardless. Even if American students were the best trained, it is almost intuitive that in the quest for large companies to be economically competitive they are going to search for not necessarily the best trained workers but the lowest compensated who can meet their needs. Despite the business agenda, it is important to ensure that American students are well educated and prepared for life because it is a moral and ethical responsibility of society.

It is important for educators and other leaders interested in improving their profession to consider triangulating the historical reform in education and the concept of compliance, tracing the research on leadership to the point where it may now be more important to understand the followers and the contextual situation, and offering a conceptual overview of innovation. Understanding the history of education reforms will provide the building blocks and essential knowledge about what is needed to reach a higher level of reform planning. Leadership is considered critically important for effective schools and businesses, but the current concept of school leadership needs to be more consistent with emerging leadership theory, which suggests that everyone in the school can be a leader depending on the task. You can't innovate without visualizing or creating mental models of truly transformational ideas. These ideas cannot be constrained by mental barriers that have been constructed culturally and institutionally over many years.

Kevin Spacey played an interesting character in the movie *K-PAX* (Softley, 2001). He claims he is from the planet K-PAX, and he offers quite a few pieces of evidence demonstrating that he can do things a typical human being from Earth cannot do. Despite his ability to do these things, most people around him refuse to believe that he is from another planet. In one of the more compelling exchanges in the movie, Spacey says to his psychiatrist, who is attempting to convince him that he is not from K-PAX, that he will consider the idea that he might not be from K-PAX if the doctor will consider the possibility that he *is* from K-PAX. That exchange is an important metaphor for educators. NCLB has been highly criticized because it requires all students to be proficient by the year 2014. This criticism, while intuitively justifiable, stems from a cultural mindset that says it is impossible. But what if there were a different mindset that said with innovation and commitment it just might be possible? What if President John F. Kennedy had never said we would put a man on the moon before the end of the decade? Innovation might empower educators to do things they don't believe possible.

The recent historic involvement of the federal government in helping the private sector solve a serious financial problem certainly provides plenty of ammunition for educators who have long decried the lack of funding for solving some of the most challenging teaching dilemmas for a very diverse student learning population. While it may have seemed acceptable to federal officials to say there wasn't enough money available or the votes weren't there to come to the aid of education, in the course of several weeks Congress mustered enough bipartisan support to spend over seven hundred billion dollars to address a national financial crisis. Educators have been hearing for a long time that there is a crisis in U.S. education and that it is essential to enact reforms to make this country's students internationally competitive and well prepared for the 21st-century workforce. It is easy to argue that the same model used to address the business/financial crisis should be used for education. While it sounds harsh, I believe that if there is any seriousness to what is being said about the importance of education, then enforcing federal compliance with evidence-based accountability, providing high-quality training for leaders, and stimulating innovation should all be accomplished with a similar model that was used for the financial "meltdown." The one-time stimulus funds, without assurance of sustaining the funding, especially in schools that are improving, will unlikely be able to continue their progress.

Let me conclude by offering an insightful comment that my friend Jerry Citron, an attorney, made when discussing this book with me. Jerry listened intently as I explained why I was writing the book, noting that I really hoped it would be used as the first step for discussion groups seriously thinking about leading effectively to meet the daunting challenges of compliance with state and federal laws, while understanding the need to be innovative for a 21st-century education organization. As only an attorney could, Jerry said, "You need to tell the readers that if they aren't serious about doing the things you are suggesting, then the book really isn't for them." After thinking about it, I agree with his point. I sincerely believe in public education but know that significant changes need to occur for the United States to be able to meet the needs of its diverse students. Those needs will require being able to comply with very challenging laws, implementing a new and different type of leadership in schools, and creating the conditions that produce innovations that result in dramatic improvement on an ongoing basis. I know that many educators are working diligently under difficult circumstances to give their students the opportunities they need to be successful. So in line with what Jerry said, I hope you will continue reading and then organize a group of colleagues to discuss how you can do a better job complying, leading, and innovating.

1

Compliance

NCLB has produced systemic change in this country, and it is fundamental. And the reason you are hearing so much moaning and groaning, at least initially and still a little, is because it is a systemic change and the people that were comfortable with the old system who were getting a lot of money and no accountability are finding themselves having to be accountable. Parents are getting information they never got, and hard questions are being asked by the teachers about what and how we are teaching. The results aren't in completely yet, but the movement is occurring. There is a significant move to teach kids in elementary school how to read and learn how to do math. If you give kids those skills, you have come pretty far down the road toward them being productive citizens and getting a successful start in life.

—Senator Judd Gregg, personal communication,
June 12, 2007, on whether No Child Left Behind was
working for the nation and, in particular, New Hampshire.
His response was relevant to that particular time.

AUTHOR'S NOTE

The interview quotations used in this book are written almost verbatim from the members of Congress and the others whom I interviewed. They have been edited or "polished" to make them more coherent but still reflect their own words. I made a decision to incorporate the comments of the interviews almost exactly in the context of our conversation so that readers would have the opportunity to hear more accurately what was said in the words of the person being interviewed. Please understand that is why, at times, the comments may wander; the respondents often reflected on other topics from the interview while we were talking. Each of the people interviewed was very cooperative and carefully reflected on what was being discussed. I believe their contributions to this book are the unique opportunity to hear the responses in their own words.

INTRODUCTION

Compliance is a way of life. When you leave your driveway and begin driving to wherever you are going, you obey speed limits and a host of other traffic laws. If you travel by airplane, you go through a thorough and daunting screening process imposed by the federal government. By April 15 every year, you spend countless hours filing your federal and state income tax returns. The simple fact of life is that while there are some individual choices in the daily lives of Americans, there are still numerous compliance requirements that are inescapable. Realistically, we simply deal with them. Just consider the number of federal government agencies and the number of regulations they promulgate and how you comply with them every day. The list seems almost endless, and it extends from the medications you use to the design of your car and so on.

Such is the case with educators and their work. It is also true for business leaders despite the perception of many educators that policymakers tend to force compliance unfairly only on them. For example, at about the same time that Congress passed the No Child Left Behind Act (NCLB), it also passed the Sarbanes-Oxley Act (SOX). Signed into law by President George W. Bush on July 30, 2002, SOX imposed costly financial reporting and governance requirements on businesses because companies like Enron, Tyco, and WorldCom engaged in highly unethical and illegal financial practices. SOX was intended to reform those egregious business practices. (For a more detailed description of this law, see Lander, 2004.)

It is important to mention SOX in a discussion about compliance for educators in order to offer a broader perspective on how federal laws can impose compliance on both business and education in very serious ways. Many such regulations have come about as the result of both education and business not taking some action to correct problems that were known to be in need of attention. In education, not enough was being done to improve the academic achievement of disadvantaged students via federal funding and ensuring that qualified teachers were teaching those students. In business, unethical and illegal corporate actions necessitated an intervention to bring about significant change in corporate governance and accountability.

> In the case of SOX, it was a response to a meltdown of the system when you had Enron and WorldCom go bankrupt, put people out of work, lose their life savings. In the case of NCLB there was recognition that the status quo wasn't satisfactory—if the federal government, like it or not, became involved in education it was important that standards be set. And I think that is where we are headed. **(Former Congressman Mike Oxley, personal communication, October 7, 2007, on whether there is a point when it is essential for the federal government to intercede in circumstances such as improper financial conduct or low student achievement)**

In 2001, the U.S. Congress passed the most intrusive federal education law ever imposed on states and local school districts. Despite the fact that education is not mentioned in the U.S. Constitution, since 1965 when the first Elementary and Secondary Education Act was passed, federal officials have gradually carved out a position for a federal role in education. That role has since grown, both financially and in terms of policy control over states and local school districts.

> I would prefer that we didn't impose federal compliance on educators and that all student needs were being met at the local level. But federal compliance is often necessary to ensure that schools are accountable for ensuring that students will have an opportunity to be successful in the 21st-century workforce. Congress needed to mandate expectations to ensure that states would use federal funding to target students with the greatest need. **(Congressman Rush Holt, personal communication, May 8, 2008)**

NCLB took federal funding and policy compliance to a new level. Significant resistance has come from some educators and professional organizations, state education officials, state policymakers, and some members of Congress, but the law has endured without much change. Yet some federal policymakers, albeit a minority, simply don't believe they should be imposing compliance requirements on states and local school districts.

> It is not the business of the federal government to be involved in local education, period. **(Congressman Donald Manzullo, personal communication, July, 25, 2007)**

Despite the fact that there are those who oppose NCLB and some who offer valid arguments that some of its provisions need revision, Congress did not take action in 2007 or 2008 to reauthorize the law when it was expected to do so. And it is unlikely that Congress will take any action to reauthorize it in 2010 either. Changes that have been made are the result of actions taken by the U.S. secretary of education, not technical corrections or reauthorization by lawmakers. Yet some believe the secretary does not have the authority to take such action and impose new compliance requirements that will potentially be changed when Congress does take action to reauthorize the law.

WHY PASS NCLB?

Why did Congress pass NCLB? That is a question asked by many. Over the last 50 or so years, since the Soviet Union launched Sputnik, numerous commissions, reports, and studies have called for substantial education reform in the United States. For the most part, those calls resulted in little change and no demonstrable improvement in achievement of U.S. students compared to their international peers or on the National Assessment of Education Progress (NAEP). Further, there is a substantial achievement gap between Caucasian students and those of color and those who live in poverty. Some reports have suggested that there is a serious disparity in the quality of teaching that students receive and that in many schools disadvantaged youth get a disproportionate number of less experienced and less qualified teachers. Those problems, coupled with a high dropout rate of high school students, resulted in Congress, with a significant bipartisan majority, passing NCLB in December 2001 and imposing strict compliance provisions on states and schools.

> It is absolutely critical that you have a federal law that requires compliance. The history of the education system at the local, state, and even to some extent the federal level demonstrates there is a great amount of energy that is used to game the system. You can see it in how they calculated graduation rates over the last several years—they are not consistent, they are not honest—for the purpose of giving the community and parents an accurate look and assessment of that school and how those students are doing. **(Congressman George Miller, personal communication, May 1, 2008)**

It is unlikely that Congress would have imposed such rigid accountability measures as those found in NCLB if states and local school districts had shown more interest in school reform over the last half century. That interest could have been exemplified by the states and districts embracing some of the transformational ideas that were proposed, improving student achievement, narrowing the achievement gap, and ensuring better qualified and experienced teacher distribution in all classrooms. The harsh tone of NCLB and its bipartisan support for rigid compliance was the result of many years of pent up frustration over a lack of success in programs funded with federal dollars. Thus, education leaders were confronted with a significant compliance leadership challenge.

> Congress is a responsive body. We're not very good at predicting future crises and then stalling them ahead of time. As a matter of fact, we're not good at that at all. I don't know anybody that is. But what we are good at is responding to our constituents, and our constituents were outraged by what they were seeing and hearing virtually every day about meltdowns of those institutions. **(Former Congressman Mike Oxley, personal communication, October 9, 2007, on why Congress sensed a need for SOX)**

CALLS FOR REFORM PRIOR TO NCLB

This section details some of the more compelling reports, commissions, and events proposed over the last half century before passage of NCLB. They provide a context for better understanding why compliance with the fundamental principles of NCLB was considered essential. (For a more comprehensive review of the calls for reform, see Kimmelman, 2006.)

Sputnik—1957

Until 1957, education in the United States was the sole responsibility of the states. Yet when the Soviet Union launched the first space satellite, Sputnik, on October 4, 1957, President Dwight Eisenhower called for training more scientists and engineers. In 1958, Congress passed the National Defense Education Act (NDEA). Using national security as the basis for the law, Congress determined that the problem with the United States falling behind the Soviet Union was the result of the education system, particularly in terms of mathematics and science. Interestingly, there are some parallel issues with the enactment of NDEA and NCLB. First, in both instances there was concern about the federal government's involvement in public education. This issue was overcome because new funds were an attractive incentive for schools to accept reforms. Second, the primary themes surrounding passage of NDEA were the space race and rocketry, but teachers had little knowledge about them or the teaching resources required to integrate them into the curriculum. Sound familiar?

Since Sputnik, the federal government has become more involved in public education. With NCLB it is using funding and compliance to force schools to improve or face sanctions. And the emphasis is still on mathematics and science education. There is a real need to offer more support to school administrators and teachers so that they understand NCLB and gain skills in the use of data, standards-based instruction, and evidence-based pedagogy in order to ensure student learning success.

Elementary and Secondary Education Act of 1965

If NDEA laid the cornerstone for federal involvement in public education, then the Elementary and Secondary Education Act of 1965 (ESEA) built the house. ESEA was part of President Lyndon Johnson's Great Society program, and its basic purpose was to provide assistance to children from low-income families. Throughout the years, federal funding for schools has continued to increase, and these funds are serving more than just children from low-income families.

Despite the increase in federal funding, students from low-income families continue to do poorly in school. During the past 50 years, these students have fallen further behind their more affluent, suburban peers. It is this achievement gap that ultimately led to the sanctions-based concept of NCLB and the move to disaggregate student achievement data by subgroup. The idea that no child could be left behind is monitored by requiring achievement data on the performance of the student subgroups. Schools that fail to meet proficiency standards first have an opportunity to improve, but ultimately could be reconstituted with a new principal and staff.

> NCLB came as the result of numerous reauthorizations of ESEA that had no teeth in them, and as a result we spent about $85 billion of taxpayer money with little result—we still have the same gap as when we started between minority and Anglo students, so NCLB was passed because of that. It has had positive results and is making a difference and narrowing the gap between haves and have-nots. Compliance, I guess, is very important, but I would rather see local school boards and states striving more for perfection rather than basic compliance. **(Congressman Howard "Buck" McKeon, personal communication, February 27, 2008)**

A Nation at Risk—1983

In 1983, U.S. Secretary of Education Terrell Bell released *A Nation at Risk: The Imperative for Educational Reform* (National Commission on Excellence in Education, 1983). This report was based on the findings from the National Commission on Excellence in Education, which Bell had created to help define the problems with U.S. education and to recommend solutions.

A quote in the report summarizes the seriousness of the problem according to the commission: "Our society is being eroded by a rising tide of mediocrity that threatens our very future as a nation and a people" (p. 5). Again, similar to what happened in 1958 with NDEA, education was being cited as the reason for the United States being confronted with serious problems. If the quality of education was not improved, there would be consequences in the future. The commission that issued this report was composed of prestigious and influential people, including representatives from business, higher education, state education agencies, and K–12 education. Although it had the bully pulpit of the secretary of education, the report did not inspire much education reform to be undertaken.

Another quote from the report is also significant: "If an unfriendly foreign power had attempted to impose on America the mediocre educational performance that exists today, we might well have viewed it as an act of war" (National Commission on Excellence in Education, 1983, p. 5). The report includes a number of indicators of the risks that would befall the country if there was no support for the commission's recommendations, including unfavorable comparisons of U.S. student achievement with their international peers, a great number of functionally illiterate teenagers and adults, declining achievement of high school students on standardized achievement tests, and concerns of business and military leaders about the costs of remedial education for the students they would have to hire or recruit. The report called for the following:

- There should be increased high school graduation requirements.
- Schools, colleges, and universities should adopt more rigorous and measurable standards and have higher expectations for academic performance and student conduct.
- Significantly more time should be devoted to the learning of the new basics, perhaps by extending the school day and year.
- There should be improved teacher preparation, and teaching should be made more rewarding and respected.
- Citizens should hold their elected officials and educators responsible for providing the leadership necessary to achieve these recommendations.

Many of the ideas and recommendations contained in *A Nation at Risk* are also included in NCLB:

- High schools need to maintain data on their graduation rates.
- States must write academic standards and administer assessments to measure whether students are meeting them.
- There are sanctions for schools that fail to meet certain progress requirements for students, including provisions stipulating that teachers and principals can be removed from the schools that do not meet them.

- Improved professional development for principals and teachers must be implemented based on practices that have evidence of success.

Although there is scant evidence that the depth of the reforms called for in *A Nation at Risk* actually were adopted prior to NCLB, it is clear that policymakers conceptually incorporated some of the recommendations from it in NCLB. The fact that Congress and the president called for rigid enforcement of NCLB was also an indication that they were taking seriously the message from *A Nation at Risk* regarding the mediocrity of U.S. education.

1989 President's Education Summit

Prior to 1989, President Ronald Reagan had tried to abolish the Department of Education; that effort failed. Not long after George H. W. Bush became president, he convened governors, some members of his cabinet, and a few high-level administration officials for an education summit. Although the process was bipartisan, it was not always amicable. Interestingly, one of the leaders of the summit was former Arkansas governor and future president Bill Clinton. The 1989 summit, citing *A Nation at Risk*, took things to another level by promoting national education goals. Of significance is the fact that the federal role in education was continuing to increase, with greater involvement in state and local policies and even suggested national education goals. At the summit, President Bush and the nation's governors agreed to the following:

- establish a process for setting national education goals
- seek greater flexibility and enhanced accountability in the use of federal resources to meet the goals, through both regulatory and legislative changes
- undertake a major state-by-state effort to restructure the education system
- report annually on progress in achieving the goals

The participants went on to agree that a task force overseen by the National Governors' Association would work with the president's designees to recommend goals by 1990. The framework for the goals would, if achieved, guarantee that the United States would be internationally competitive in several areas:

- the readiness of children to start school
- student performance on international achievement tests, especially in math and science

- reduction of the dropout rate and improvement of academic performance, especially among at-risk students
- the functional literacy of American adults
- the level of training necessary to guarantee a competitive workforce
- the supply of qualified teachers and up-to-date technology
- establishment of safe, disciplined, and drug-free schools

Furthermore, the summit concluded that states must focus on the achievement of all students, raise academic standards, and be responsible for improving them. It was time to put rhetoric behind us and focus on action. Many of the summit's recommendations are included in NCLB—dropout rate reduction, safe schools, qualified teachers, performance assessment, and higher standards. Despite the fact that the president convened this summit and governors from both parties participated, the results were similar to those obtained in the past—very little was done by educators to address concerns raised at the summit. The simple fact was that the education profession was consistently being advised of potentially serious problems by people who could enact new education policy. Unfortunately, educators did not do enough to address their concerns.

Goals 2000—1994

There is some irony in the fact that President George H.W. Bush, a Republican, convened the 1989 President's Education Summit, which was cochaired by Arkansas Governor Bill Clinton, a Democrat, who then defeated Bush in the 1993 presidential election. One cornerstone of President Clinton's domestic agenda was education. Emboldened by the reauthorization of ESEA, also known as Goals 2000, a law containing a number of principles from the summit convened by President Bush, President Clinton appointed the former governor of South Carolina, Richard Riley, to be his secretary of education. Goals 2000 set national goals that called for the following:

- school readiness
- school completion
- student academic achievement
- leadership in mathematics and science
- adult literacy
- safe and drug-free schools

Although most of the goals were topics that historically addressed education issues regarding student achievement, the list added safe and drug-free schools. This issue was rather new to the debate and only added to the tasks with which schools were already struggling. Goals 2000 was the forerunner to NCLB and became its cornerstone. Congress and President Clinton had set the stage for more federal involvement in state and local education policy.

1996 National Education Summit

Governors from more than 40 states met with national business leaders on March 26 and 27, 1996, to discuss the state of U.S. education. It was the sense of many of the nation's business leaders that the education system was in need of significant change, and since educators had not taken it upon themselves to make that change, the task would fall to others who would. The summit was led by Louis Gerstner, then chairman and CEO of IBM. Of note is the fact that no education organizations were invited to participate in this summit. The briefing materials provided background on seven key questions:

1. Why do we need high academic standards?
2. Does the public support high academic standards and accountability?
3. Does the business community support high academic standards and accountability?
4. Do other nations have academic standards, and is the United States competitive?
5. What exactly is a standard?
6. How much progress has been made by the states in their efforts to implement high academic standards, assessment, and accountability?
7. How can technology be an effective tool to help students and schools reach high academic standards?

These questions clearly delineated the troublesome trends in education that had been emerging for a long time and the emphasis that business leaders and governors were going to place on them to ensure that changes took place in state education systems. It was apparent that standards, assessment, and accountability—key provisions of NCLB—and international comparisons of student achievement would be used to determine how well U.S. students were doing in core subjects.

In addition, how technology could effectively be implemented to improve the process of education was going to continue to receive attention from these individuals, who believed they could actually make changes in a system that had been resisting them for many years. The governors and business leaders left the summit recommending that there be clear academic standards and better subject matter content at the state and local levels. No longer were they viewing U.S. education as separate and distinct by states; they were now working within a national paradigm.

National Commission on Teaching and America's Future—1996

The National Commission on Teaching and America's Future operated on the basis of three premises:

1. What teachers know and can do is the most important influence on what students learn.

2. Recruiting, preparing, and retaining good teachers is the central strategy to improving schools.

3. School reform cannot succeed unless it focuses on creating the conditions under which teachers can teach and teach well.

The commission set a goal for implementation of its recommendations by 2006. What was particularly eye opening was what the commission saw as the barriers to achieving its recommendations: low expectations for student performance, unenforced standards for teachers, major flaws in teacher preparation, painfully slipshod teacher recruitment, inadequate induction for beginning teachers, lack of professional development and rewards for knowledge and skill, and schools that were structured for failure rather than success. Again, the themes were eerily similar to previous calls for reform, with nothing new being added to the proposals:

- Get serious about standards for both students and teachers.
- Reinvent teacher preparation and professional development.
- Fix teacher recruitment, and put qualified teachers in every classroom.
- Encourage and reward teacher knowledge and skill.
- Create schools that are organized for student and teacher success.

However, one noteworthy aspect of this commission was its complete and total focus on teaching. All of its recommendations and acknowledged barriers reinforced what had been said about the problems with U.S. education for many years.

1999 National Education Summit

The 1999 National Education Summit included approximately 30 governors, business executives, and educators, and it focused on three core principles:

1. Reform begins with a commitment to set the highest academic standards.

2. Quality assessments are essential to measure progress against those standards.

3. Implementation of comprehensive systems is required to guarantee full accountability for results, starting with real improvements in student achievement.

The participants at this summit affirmed their commitment to raising student achievement to world-class standards. They also set a six-month deadline for states to respond to the summit action statement urging progress on the following key challenges:

- improved educator quality
- helping all students achieve high standards
- strengthened accountability

It is apparent that the gradual and consistent evolution of the call for rigorous academic standards, accountability for meeting them, and improved teacher quality were gaining a foothold with an increasing number of people, and those people had the power and influence to enact change. To improve educator quality, the participants committed to doing the following:

- strengthen entrance and exit requirements of teacher education programs
- target professional development programs that give teachers the content knowledge and skills to teach to higher standards
- develop competitive salary structures to attract and retain the best qualified teachers and school leaders with pay for skills and performance

To help all students achieve high standards, the participants agreed to work together in states to ensure that every school had a rigorous curriculum and professional development program aligned with state standards and tests, expand public school choice and charter schools, and develop extended-day and extended-year programs for students at risk. To strengthen accountability, they also agreed to work together in states to create incentives for success and consequences for failure, strengthen the ability of principals and teachers to select their own colleagues and control school budgets, provide students at risk of failure with opportunities for extra help, and recognize highly successful schools and intervene in low-performing schools.

These commitments were all significant parts of NCLB, too. It would be logical to conclude that the work of the 1999 National Education Summit had a significant influence on the law. For educators, the summit's recommendations should have served as notice that policymakers were getting more serious about what they believed were needed reforms with respect to the weaknesses in U.S. education and that more should have been undertaken to address them.

National Commission on Mathematics and Science Teaching for the 21st Century—2000

In 1999, Secretary of Education Richard Riley appointed a commission to make recommendations for improving mathematics and science teaching in the 21st century. Since Sputnik, there had been a steady stream of reports calling for improvements in U.S. student achievement in both of these subjects. The National Commission on Mathematics and Science Teaching, known as the Glenn Commission (named for its chairman, former astronaut and then Ohio Senator John Glenn), of which I was a member, began its work with the knowledge that student achievement in mathematics and science was far from acceptable after reviewing students' performance on the Third International Mathematics and Science Study (TIMSS). TIMSS provided data demonstrating that the longer U.S. students remained in school, the more their performance declined in mathematics and science compared with students in other countries.

Although U.S. students did fairly well in both subjects in Grade 4, their performance declined considerably by the time they reached Grades 8 and 12. The Glenn Commission identified four key points (U.S. Department of Education, 2000). First, the commission was convinced that the future well-being of the nation and its people depends not just on how well we educate our children generally, but also specifically on how well we educate them in mathematics and science. Once again, the future of the nation was included in a major education report citing the importance of education in solving a critical national problem.

Second, it was abundantly clear from the evidence that the system was not doing the job that it should do—or could do—in teaching children to understand and use ideas from these fields. The Glenn Commission actually reemphasized much of what *Life* magazine wrote in its 1958 series "A Crisis in Education."

Third, after an extensive, in-depth review of what was happening in U.S. classrooms, the commission concluded that the most powerful instrument for change, and therefore the place to begin, was the very core of education: teaching. Very few reports prior to this, with the exception of that of the 1999 National Education Summit and a few others, addressed the importance of teaching in their recommendations. During the previous 40 years, there was minimal change in teacher preparation programs and ongoing learning opportunities in professional development for teachers, despite the increasing complexity of actually teaching mathematics and science.

Fourth, the commission believed that committing to reach three specific goals could go far in bringing about the needed basic changes in the nation. The goals went directly to the issues of quality, quantity, and an enabling work environment for teachers of mathematics and science:

1. Establish an ongoing system to improve the quality of mathematics and science teaching in Grades K–12.

2. Increase significantly the number of mathematics and science teachers, and improve the quality of their preparation.

3. Improve the working environment, and make the teaching profession more attractive for K–12 mathematics and science teachers.

The Glenn Commission's report clearly outlined a plan for science, technology, engineering, and mathematics education, a topic of considerable interest currently with policymakers and business leaders. While the report received widespread publicity, the administration of President George W. Bush chose not to implement its recommendations.

2001 National Education Summit

The 2001 National Education Summit was held in October, despite the catastrophic events of the September 11 terrorist attacks having taken place so recently. The fact that the summit was held affirms the serious commitment the participants had for reforming U.S. education and their belief that a healthy public education system is the foundation of the country's democracy.

Like the compelling statements in 1957 about the security of the United States after the launch of Sputnik and those in 1983's *A Nation at Risk* about society being eroded, the 2001 National Education Summit began with an affirmation that U.S. education was an important part of creating national success in a global environment and its decline was a serious problem for the country. This summit was the third time in five years that prestigious policymakers and corporate executives had gathered to discuss education. Certainly, the fact that they were devoting so much time and attention to education was a clear signal that significant policy changes to reform public education were on the way. Indeed, not long after this summit, President George W. Bush and a bipartisan leadership group from Congress met to finalize NCLB. The rationale for the 2001 summit was to support the goal of high standards. The participants' briefing book acknowledged that although there were examples of schools turning things around, the goal of high standards for all had not been met.

They also acknowledged that the president and Congress were poised to enact legislation that would accelerate the pace of the reforms they were recommending. Interestingly, they noted that states were working hard but would have to work even harder in the coming months and years. The three primary focuses of this summit were public support, teaching, and learning as it related to closing the achievement gap and using data to drive improvement from testing and accountability. With respect to the belief that there was public opposition to standards and testing, the participants at the summit were told that the claims were overblown. Their report noted that testing represented a minor investment of time for a worthwhile goal. They affirmed their belief that schools needed to use standards to raise achievement and not narrow instruction. Their support for standards was based on the notion that higher standards would raise expectations for student learning. Furthermore, they believed testing would be the best way to measure progress toward attaining the standards.

To close the achievement gap, the summit participants cited a number of requirements that researchers had identified as characteristics of successful schools:

- a relentless focus on academic performance for all students
- a shared sense among faculty and staff that they are all responsible for the learning of every student
- frequent and regular assessment of student progress for diagnostic purposes
- principals who are true instructional leaders
- flexible use of time

Summit participants discussed how states could improve instruction by creating a supportive policy environment, and their recommendations were clearly aligned with the provisions that would be contained in NCLB. First, they called for clear, measurable standards that would give appropriate guidance to all stakeholders. Another familiar part of the discussion was the use of disaggregated assessment data, ultimately a provision in NCLB that has become quite controversial. The report from the summit said that it would be essential to disaggregate testing data by race/ethnicity, income, special education status, and limited English proficiency. It noted that simply knowing that a certain percentage of students in a school meet standards can hide differences among students that may never be remedied.

Finally, the summit emphasized the importance of attracting and retaining qualified educators. Participants discussed the fact that too often the students who need the best teachers are taught by those teachers who have the least experience and qualifications. To close the achievement gap, that problem had to be rectified.

Professional development also received considerable attention. Summit participants recognized that the movement toward standards-based, assessment-driven education reform would require professional learning opportunities for teachers. Interestingly, they noted that in other professions (e.g., law, medicine), such opportunities are provided routinely. In addition, they mentioned that onetime workshops were not the answer and that educational professional development was often ineffective because it was delivered in ineffective ways.

The 2001 National Education Summit recommendations were the closest to modeling what would ultimately become NCLB. This last summit brought together the concepts that became the fundamental underpinnings of the law.

No Child Left Behind Act—2001

I think there is more than ever, but as I said, we don't want to be a national board. Our system is failing. I think we rank 28th on an international assessment, and there are many countries that surpass us on student performance. The only way we will stay ahead of the developing countries is to continue to have the creativity and innovation we have had to stay a step ahead of them. We are seeing a loss of patents, scientific papers, and prizes given in the international community. I don't want to have a school system like China that runs 24 hours a day, 7 days a week practically, but I think we have to instill in our children the love of learning, how important it is, and how they could benefit from their education. **(Former Speaker of the House Dennis Hastert, personal communication, August 7, 2007, on whether there is an important federal role in education)**

In January 2002, President George W. Bush signed into law NCLB, the most comprehensive federal education law ever written and one that imposed serious sanctions for states and schools that failed to abide by its provisions. It was clear that our nation's leading policymakers, both Democrats and Republicans, were serious about ensuring that schools would improve the achievement of their students. Arguably, the real goal is for schools to improve and base their improvement work on products, practices, and programs that have evidence showing that they work.

It wasn't as necessary in the case of Florida because we started our journey a little bit earlier than NCLB, the act itself. I ran the campaign of 1998, which was about what we called the A+ program, that had many similarities to the accountability measures of NCLB. So the national imperatives of having it as a national law and having some teeth to it I thought were important. In our particular case, it didn't have much of an impact. But it could have probably been a little harder around the edge in terms of the accountability elements of the law. **(Former Florida Governor Jeb Bush, personal communication, July 20, 2009)**

NCLB incorporates concepts that had been discussed for many years and imposes sanctions for failing to meet certain requirements. Clearly, the law incorporates accountability, assessment, academic standards, and teacher quality as its cornerstones. All four of these concepts have been subjects of concern in nearly every report on education since 1957. A quote from a *USA Today* opinion piece captures this national sense of school reform as it relates to federal law:

> At a time when the nation's primary driver of school reform—the No Child Left Behind law—is caught up in presidential politics, it's a case study in how to succeed. It should also prod educators to move ahead, not wait to see how No Child Left Behind will change once Congress renews it. ("Our View on Improving Schools," 2007, para. 2)

SOME ADDITIONAL REPORTS—POST-NCLB

Education has been the subject of considerable debate since NCLB became law in 2002. What is striking is the number of new voices emerging in the debate on how to improve public education. The Internet age has spawned countless blogs that have encouraged discussions with many diverse opinions on just about every education issue. New special interest organizations have emerged, and there has been much more active policy involvement from organizations that traditionally did not devote much time and attention to policy advocacy. For example, the Association for Supervision and Curriculum Development and the National Staff Development Council are now actively involved in policy advocacy. Prior to NCLB these organizations were more centrally focused on their specific missions of curriculum and staff development. There is little doubt today that the education practitioner's voice is being heard from more organizations and that those organizations have a better understanding of the implications of the federal role in education and what compliance with it means to them.

I include here discussion of some post-NCLB reports that emphasize a variety of truly different proposals and focus on the workforce because the current education theme is for the United States to be more competitive and to train a different type of workforce for the 21st century. However, I maintain that as with the pre-NCLB reports and commissions, the newer calls for reform, if unheeded, will grow and the compliance issues for educators will become even more challenging. I am not implying that educators should merely fall in line and comply with these proposals. But there is a substantial need to engage in a thorough discussion of whether some of them could result in a better education system and do more to make students and the nation more successful in the new global economy. The theme of change needs to be embraced by educators, particularly in situations where the model they are using is not producing satisfactory results.

Overall, I got the sense from just about every member of Congress whom I interviewed that there is a preference not to promulgate laws that require compliance. However, it was their belief that, without the sanctions included in NCLB, there would be no sense of urgency among educators to attain loftier goals.

> I would say that what we learned about NCLB is that we were very effective on the front end and that setting standards, and measuring performance against those standards, and creating data on student performance works. We have been much less effective in turning around struggling schools as we identify them. I would say absolutely we need to stay true to this idea that you will have standards, you will measure against those standards, and you will transparently report your progress with all children in reaching them. Where I have less confidence at this point is in predetermining solutions. **(Gary Huggins, personal communication, September 23, 2008)**

The New Workforce—2005

Much of the criticism directed at education has come from the business community. Whether valid or not, representatives from business have become more active in education policymaking. The American Management Association issued a brief (Buhler, 2005; based on Hankin, 2005) on the five sweeping trends that will shape a company's future, which have implications for educators in terms of both curriculum and human resource planning:

1. *The aging population:* Seniors are working longer and staying in their communities. Life expectancy for men is just over 78 years and for women 82; ultimately, life expectancy could exceed 120 years.

2. *The growth in different household types:* "It is no longer effective for companies to provide one-size-fits-all benefits to meet everyone's needs. With more diverse households, companies must offer more flexible benefits to better meet the needs of all the participants in their workforce" (Buhler, 2005, p. 4).

3. *Generations:* Today's workforce is composed of four different generations, and these differences create complex challenges. The Silent Generation refers to the workers born between 1922 and 1945. The Baby Boomers were born between 1946 and 1964. Those in Generation X were born between 1965 and 1976. And finally,

Generation Y refers to those born between 1977 and 2000. Each generation is identified with unique characteristics that employers need to understand.

4. *Increasing diversity:* Diversity in the workplace can be challenging because companies have to confront issues such as acceptance, flexibility, and respect and create cultures in which the differences simply don't matter.

5. *Trust, respect, and ethics:* "The benefits of companies supporting a higher purpose include better morale, more commitment, more productivity, lower turnover, less stress and better financial performance" (p. 7). This trend is likely a response to the rationale that necessitated Congress passing SOX.

Tough Choices or Tough Times—2007

Tough Choices or Tough Times (National Center on Education and the Economy, 2007) offers some bold and truly nontraditional goals that call for a total overhaul of U.S. education by 2021. I include these recommendations here because they are very different from some of the calls for reform that were less dramatic and bold, have the support of a diverse but influential group of people, and would not easily gain acceptance from those who would be charged with their implementation.

Of particular significance is the composition of the bipartisan commission that drafted the recommendations. The members represented policymakers, special interest groups, higher education, K–12 education, and business. For example, two recent former U.S. secretaries of education, Richard Riley and Roderick Paige, appointed by a Democratic and Republican president, respectively, served on the commission. Joel Klein, Tom Payzant, and Clifford Janey, also members, all led major U.S. city school systems.

Gaining consensus from a diverse group on this bold set of proposals is unusual in education:

1. *Revamp the high school–college transition:* This recommendation calls for ending high school for most students after 10th grade and having students take rigorous state board exams to determine what they should be able to do to succeed in college. Students who do well on the exams would go directly to technical schools and colleges. Those who don't could stay in high school for additional preparation for the exams.

2. *Reallocate funds to high-priority strategies for improving system performance:* The report suggests that the new progression through high school would save approximately $60 billion that could be used to improve preparation for students to attend college.

3. *Offer pre-K for all:* Some of the savings from the second recommendation would be used to provide high-quality education for all four-year-olds and all low-income three-year-olds.

4. *Redesign how schools are funded:* Some of the savings from the second recommendation would be used to provide funds to schools serving low-income and disadvantaged students. This recommendation also calls for abolishing local funding and requiring states to raise and distribute funds for schools.

5. *Redesign how schools are managed:* All public schools would be managed by independent contractors operating under performance contracts managed by local school districts. Only those that demonstrate results for improving student achievement would be funded, and parents could send their children to any school they choose.

6. *Educate the current workforce to a high standard:* Adults currently in the workforce would have the right to return to school for a free education comparable to the new high school plan proposed in the report.

7. *Create personal competitiveness accounts:* The federal government would deposit $500 for every child at birth, and the account would allow people to receive ongoing education and training throughout their lives.

A Test of Leadership—2006

With so much emphasis being placed on the preparation and ongoing development of teachers, it seems appropriate to include a summary of the findings and recommendations from a commission on higher education appointed by then U.S. Secretary of Education Margaret Spellings (U.S. Department of Education, 2006). While K–12 education has borne the brunt of most criticisms directed at educators and ideas about how the system should be reformed, clearly higher education will have to play a role in how those who lead and teach in the schools are trained. The following are some of the commission's key recommendations:

- K–12 school systems and state policymakers should collaborate to expand college participation and success by creating a seamless pathway between high school and college. Graduation standards should closely align with college and employer expectations.
- States should provide incentives for colleges to collaborate with K–12 schools to improve college preparation and persistence for underserved students.
- Students and colleges must take joint responsibility for academic success.

- Information about college that is available to students must be improved, and financial barriers to attendance must be reduced.
- Colleges should embrace a culture of continuous innovation and quality improvement by developing new pedagogies, curricula, and technologies to improve learning. This is especially important in science and mathematics.
- A national strategy for lifelong learning should be designed to citizens and the country at the forefront of the knowledge revolution.

America's Perfect Storm—2007

"Our nation is in the midst of a perfect storm—the result of the confluence of three powerful forces—that is having a considerable impact on our country" (Kirsch, Braun, & Yamamoto, 2007, p. 3). This report suggests that if policies are not changed, the United States will continue to grow apart, experiencing more inequity with respect to wages and increased social and political polarization. These are the three forces referenced in the previous quote:

1. Economic restructuring that places a premium on literacy and numeracy skills

2. Uneven distribution of these skills

3. Sweeping demographic trends that are changing the population and workforce

As *America's Perfect Storm* concludes, put simply, we can grow together or we can grow apart. Critical to growing together is acting decisively to ensure a bright, secure future for America's children and the country.

Leaders and Laggards—2007

In 2007, the Institute for a Competitive Workforce of the U.S. Chamber of Commerce issued *Leaders and Laggards: A State-by-State Report Card on Educational Effectiveness*:

It has been nearly a quarter century since the seminal report *A Nation at Risk* was issued in 1983. Since that time, a knowledge-based economy has emerged, the Internet has reshaped commerce and communication, exemplars of creative commerce like Microsoft, eBay, and Southwest Airlines have revolutionized the way we live, and the global economy has undergone wrenching change. (p. 5)

The report identified some major findings that reinforce the need to transform educational leadership and implement more innovation:

1. The return on educational investment varies greatly across states.

2. Certain states with a large percentage of low-income and minority students score far better than others on achievement tests.

3. States could do much more to ensure a 21st-century teaching workforce. They need better data on what is being done to evaluate teacher performance, to reward good teachers, to make it easier for talented candidates to compete for jobs, and to remove ineffective teachers.

4. Truth in advertising is inconsistent. Many states paint a much rosier picture of how their schools are doing than is actually the case.

5. State standards are too often inadequate. States need to establish more rigorous guidelines for what students need to learn.

6. Forward-looking states are fostering innovation.

7. High school graduation rates and college preparation levels are much higher in some states than in others.

8. States have begun to improve data collection efforts.

How the World's Best-Performing School Systems Come Out On Top—2007

Michael Barber and Mona Mourshed (2007) studied 25 school systems throughout the world, including 10 of the top-performing systems identified in the Programme for International Student Assessment (PISA). PISA measures how well 10th graders are prepared for their future life's endeavors and focuses on literacy, mathematics, and science, with an emphasis on one of those disciplines each time it is administered. The top-performing countries were Australia, Belgium, Canada, Finland, Hong Kong, Japan, the Netherlands, New Zealand, Singapore, and South Korea. The other school systems studied by Barber and Mourshed were those that demonstrated rapidly improving achievement. The U.S. school districts that they selected, which were chosen from a list of finalists for the Broad Prize for Urban Education, were Atlanta, Boston, Chicago, and New York.

Despite the differences between the school systems and districts, Barber and Mourshed found remarkable similarities with respect to what it takes to improve school performance. The most important finding, which is not surprising at all, is that "the most effective way to deliver sustained and substantial improvements in outcomes is through sustained and substantial improvements in instruction" (p. 32). This requires that high-performing schools do three basic tasks well:

1. Get the right people to become teachers. (The quality of an education system cannot exceed the quality of its teachers.)

2. Develop these people into effective instructors. (The only way to improve outcomes is to improve instruction.)

3. Put in place systems and targeted support to ensure that every child is able to benefit from excellent instruction. (The only way for the system to reach the highest performance is to raise the standard for every student.)

A Broader, Bolder Approach to Education—2008

The Economic Policy Institute (2008) convened a bipartisan task force composed of some nationally well-known and influential people who represent a variety of interests, including education, social welfare, health, housing, and civil rights. As the name of the task force implies, it calls for a broader and bolder approach to improving education for all children. The new approach does not discount the importance of formal schooling, but it does call for high-quality early childhood and preschool programs, afterschool and summer programs, and programs that develop parents' capacity to support their children's education. In addition to basic skills and cognitive growth, more emphasis needs to be placed on the development of the whole person—physical health, character, social development, and nonacademic skills—from birth through the end of formal schooling. The task force specifically noted that these new policies and practices must be supported by a "preponderance of evidence presently available from serious research" (p. 2).

One important conceptual difference in this task force's report is recognition of the need to plan for the whole child and of the importance of coordination between school and health services. "More than a half century of research, both here and abroad, has documented a powerful association between social and economic disadvantage and low student achievement" (Economic Policy Institute, 2008, p. 1). The report clearly emphasizes that doing this will be a significant challenge.

SUMMARY

Whether or not you agree with a compliance provision, once it is a law, rule, or regulation promulgated by a federal, state, or local agency with the authority to do so, the reality is that you must comply. Compliance with laws like NCLB and SOX require effective leadership for the 21st century, and that leadership will necessitate the ability to stimulate innovation if American students are to be successful in a rapidly changing, knowledge-based worldwide economy.

> I think in several key areas of society, breaking out of measuring inputs and instead measuring outputs is critical. **(Congressman Mark Kirk, personal communication, July 25, 2007)**

The fact that there are so many research studies, reports, commissions, and special interest groups only compounds what was once a relatively simple equation for education policymakers. Now that there are so many diverse voices on education representing a host of ideological think tanks, bloggers, and others, policymakers are confronted with difficult decisions about what compliance is best on a national scale. But it is also true that practitioners must be more willing to recognize the need for change and figure out how the culture of the profession and "the way we have been doing it" can be transformed to better meet the needs of students who will live in a very different world than the one in which most of us grew up. Today's students are immersed in a digital environment. They communicate socially on web sites, take classes online, and access library and news content online, and it is difficult to predict with any degree of accuracy what will be the next major transformational discovery related to accessing information and communicating.

The post-NCLB reports are all fairly consistent. They all note the presence of a new knowledge-based global economy and the need for more innovation. They emphasize the importance of looking at education more systemically in the context of pre-K to post–high school, raising the quality of teachers and teaching, improving student achievement, closing the achievement gap, and placing more emphasis on accountability and effective leadership.

Successful leaders can effectively lead in a compliance-driven environment and understand that compliance doesn't have to stifle their leadership strategies or innovative initiatives. Education leaders who choose the path of resistance often find that all of their energy is channeled into negative and unproductive efforts. They spend the majority of their time debating, complaining, and using resources inefficiently. Leaders must move beyond this mindset and identify those areas of compliance that can be advanced through their leadership in order to get their staff on board with a reform effort, garnering business and community support, making realistic changes in budgets and planning efforts, and motivating a team to meet and exceed the compliance challenge.

> We spent billions of dollars on education, and we've seen virtually no movement in the quality of education, particularly with low-income kids. Title I had become a cash flow stream in the education community with no accountability. The results should have been low-income kids being brought up to the level of their peers or at least being given the tools they need. As a former governor and conservative, I thought it was a tremendous waste of dollars and an ineffective program, and it needed to be fundamentally changed. **(Senator Judd Gregg, personal communication, June 12, 2007, on why he supported NCLB)**

DISCUSSION ACTIVITY QUESTIONS

1. How could federal compliance drive organizational transformation in schools?

2. If educators should use what they learn from the NAEP, should it drive federal compliance policies? The following figure shows reading and math scores from the first NAEP testing to the present against the backdrop of each reauthorization of ESEA. Discuss whether compliance with each reauthorization of ESEA resulted in improved student achievement.

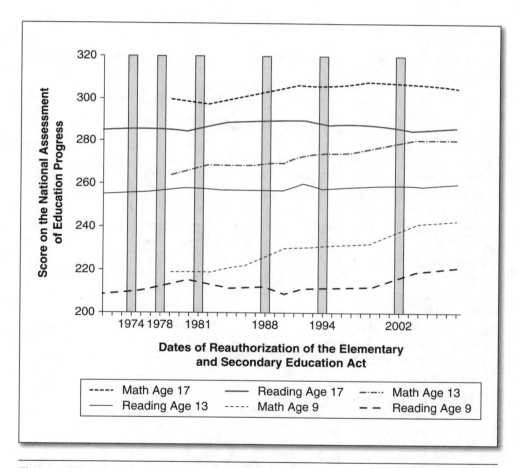

This sparkline diagram was designed by Matt Burke, at Learning Point Associates, and is based on Edward Tufte's work on visual display of quantitative information.

A sparkline is a small, data-rich graphic that can be quickly and easily interpreted. This sparkline displays over 30 years of NAEP long-term trend data from reading and math at three different age points. Each vertical bar represents a year of ESEA reauthorization.

This graphic suggests that reading scores have remained relatively stable (with the exception of age 9) while math scores have shown the most improvement over time at each age group. ESEA reauthorization appears to have had little to no effect on reading or math scores at any age.

3. What compliance laws, rules, or regulations currently impose challenging implementation requirements in your district or school? Why?

4. Federal involvement or no federal involvement? Why? Has federal involvement in education led to better teaching and learning?

HOW CAN TEACHERS AND GOVERNMENT BUILD A RELATIONSHIP TO ACHIEVE WORLD-CLASS STANDARDS?

Sir Michael Barber

At the outset, we need some understanding of what it takes to be world class. In education, we have this knowledge from a series of international benchmarking studies. What marks out the best systems in the world is that they recruit great people into teaching and invest in their skills effectively both at the start of their careers and throughout them so that they teach lessons of consistently high quality. These systems also set out with the expectation that every child can achieve high standards, and they offer extra expert help to children who fall below. *Consistency* is the key word from our point of view in the United States and England, for these same international benchmarking exercises reveal that our education systems have far too much variation from classroom to classroom and school to school. In fact, as Andreas Schleicher, who organizes the Organisation for Economic Co-operation and Development's benchmarking of school systems, says, "Few if any systems are doing more of the right things in policy terms than England's, but this has yet to translate into consistent quality at classroom level." In the United States, the challenge is greater still because, especially in large urban areas, the right policies are not yet in place.

To achieve world-class education, building this reliability is crucial, and it begins and ends in teachers' classrooms. In other words, it can only be brought about by frontline professionals who share the mission, benefit from excellent management, and are given the tools and incentives to deliver consistent high quality by an enabling government. With this background, then, the framework described in Table 1.1 can be developed as the starting point for dialogue between governments and the teaching profession. It assumes that systems have to move through three phases, from "awful" to "great."

Table 1.1 How the Relationship Between Government and Professions Could Transform Public Service

Phase of development	Awful to Adequate	Adequate to Good	Good to Great
Chief focus of system	Tackling under-performance	Improvement	World-class performance
Role of government	Prescribing	Regulating	Enabling
Role of profession	Implementing	Accommodating	Leading
Nature of relationship	Top-down and antagonistic	Negotiated and pragmatic	Principled and strategic
Time horizon	Immediate	Medium-term	Continuous
Chief outcomes	Reduced failure	Uneven improvement	Consistent quality
What citizens think	Reduced anxiety	Growing satisfaction	Active engagement

At the very least, a framework such as this could provide a common language for the dialogue. That alone would be a major improvement on talking past each other, which has seemed so common in many countries. Two factors should enable it. The first is that even when a system is awful, there are plenty of head teachers and teachers who are doing an outstanding job. Right from the outset, government needs to foster a strong relationship with those leaders who are successful. If they express impatience with the slow pace of change, it helps counterbalance the drag effect of those who want to slow things down. Indeed, this alliance with successful leaders is a key part of that process of building what Michael Fullan (2009) calls "the ever-widening circles of leadership" (p. 218). The second enabling factor is the vastly improved information available about the performance of public services. This information—everything from published performance data to the growing range of international benchmarks—provide (and in the future will provide even better) the evidence base for this conversation.

Certainly it is in everyone's interest to make the attempt to create a principled relationship between government and the teaching profession. The demand for education of real quality that is available to all is overwhelming. Those who work in education would surely prefer to be more motivated and more successful rather than less, while governments in the next decade will find they need to sign up to this vision, too, if they are to succeed in meeting bold aspirations. Without something along these lines, we are likely to see public education systems collectively—government and the school workforce—fail to implement reform successfully or communicate to the users and to those who pay for the services where they are heading and how they are doing. As a consequence, a spiral of decline could set in. If government and the teaching profession aim their messages only at each other and appear to be at loggerheads, then the public will inevitably be both skeptical and confused. The task of building and sustaining this relationship is a responsibility of the leaders in both education and the government.

[For a longer discussion of the issues raised in this short essay, see Barber, 2008.]

Used with permission of Sir Michael Barber, Founder, Education Delivery Institute, Washington, D.C.

2

Leadership

Well, I think you have to sit back and look at some of the new research or attention, in any event, to the way kids are learning in order to understand who the most effective kinds of leaders are going to be who work with them. The suggestion is team building. The best leaders are going to be the ones who know how to bring people together into that kind of team environment. They have to be people who listen well and knit together different perspectives so they can locate the common ground among a group and, in a sense, invite and encourage them to move forward.

—Congressman John Sarbanes,
personal communication, September 17, 2008

INTRODUCTION

Chapter 1 discussed the history of calls for education reform and what led to No Child Left Behind (NCLB), the most intrusive federal compliance law for education. It also discussed Sarbanes-Oxley (SOX), a law that imposed compliance requirements on business. Both laws created significant accountability responsibilities for organizational leaders to bring results to their school districts or companies and were passed by Congress at approximately the same time. In a compliance environment, for organizations to be successful there is an unarguable need for effective leadership. *Leadership* is a term that is used frequently but has different meanings to different people. One fact is certain, however: there cannot be leadership if there are no followers. And many years of research on leadership have not resulted in a single model that can be used to ensure that someone develops into an effective leader.

Yet one important fact about leadership, as Sharon Daloz Parks (2005) says, is that it can be learned:

> Within this paradigm of teaching and learning, and across every sector and profession, it is one thing to teach knowledge of the field, and it is quite another to prepare people to exercise the judgment and skill needed to bring that knowledge into the intricate system of relationships that constitute the dynamic world of practice. It is yet another challenge altogether to prepare someone to practice leadership within the profession and the communities it serves—to prepare a physician, for example, to practice leadership within a hospital system and the regional, national or world health care system as well as to care for individual patients. (p. 5)

On the back cover of the highly regarded book *The Tipping Point*, by Malcolm Gladwell (2002), the tipping point is explained as "that magic moment when an idea, trend, or social behavior crosses a threshold, tips, and spreads like wildfire." Gladwell notes that one of the distinguishing characteristics of the tipping point is that little changes can have big effects. To apply the tipping point theory, one must reframe the way one thinks about the world. Gladwell expands on that idea by discussing how people have difficulty relating to new information and estimating dramatic exponential change. Using Gladwell's theory, I would predict that education leadership could undergo the most significant transformational change that has been witnessed since traditional school leaders, superintendents, and principals prepared for their work under state licensure and traditional college preparatory programs. I predict that education leadership will undergo a transformation based on three premises:

1. Most of the attention on school leaders in the media is focused on nontraditional leaders such as Joel Klein in New York; Michelle Rhee in the District of Columbia; Paul Vallas in New Orleans, and former CEO of the Chicago Public Schools; and Arne Duncan, U.S. Secretary of Education and former CEO of the Chicago Public Schools. None of these individuals emerged through traditional school leader preparation programs. Further, Secretary Duncan has said that mayors should take control of big city school districts where there is low academic achievement ("U.S. Education Secretary to Push for Mayoral Control of Schools," 2009). That is hardly an endorsement of thousands of experienced school administrators looking to take on some of education leadership's most challenging situations.

That's a great question and a topic we are interested in. I firmly believe there will be a need for new kinds of leadership in the 21st century, and that's simply because the organization of schools has become so complex that the skills and the abilities required to be a superintendent, particularly of those very large urban school systems, require a set of skills that goes above and beyond that of the typical education leader. I can talk with experience, having been superintendent of one of the 10 largest school systems in America: Fairfax County, Virginia. But it is a very different experience. I started out as a superintendent of a district with 7,000 students. After four different superintendencies, I graduated to larger and larger systems, winding up in Fairfax County with 170,000 students. They all had the title of superintendent, but they were very different jobs." **(Dan Domenech, executive director, American Association of School Administrators, personal communication, April 22, 2009, on the tipping point I mentioned for school leadership and nontraditional leaders)**

2. The largest single federal education funding increase, the American Recovery and Reinvestment Act of 2009 (ARRA), came with strong comments from Secretary Duncan about assurances that the money was being spent by school leaders well and would bring positive results, innovation, and new ideas to school reform. He was emphatic on this point "We'll be sending you billions of dollars by month's end. Spend the money quickly but wisely. And keep receipts; we'll be asking" (Dillon, 2009, p. A14).

3. In an unprecedented move, as part of its response to the financial crisis that began in 2008, the federal government compelled General Motors to replace its CEO by threatening to withhold federal funds to help the company stay in business. In essence, federal officials didn't believe that Rick Wagoner, the longtime CEO of General Motors, could lead the company back to profitability. They believed that for the company to be internationally competitive, there were two options: Wagoner needed to leave, or GM would not receive the needed federal funds and ultimately go out of business or declare bankruptcy (King & Stoll, 2009).[1]

Alone, any of the aforementioned items might not be the tipping point. But when combined, and considering that all three occurred in a rather brief period of time, they indicate a new era for education leadership. This new era will emphasize rigorous accountability to the federal government for systemic education leadership. It is unlikely that the federal government will move away from its compliance requirements that are aligned to results as stipulated in NCLB or ARRA funding. School leaders such as superintendents and principals will be held accountable for their districts or buildings meeting challenging academic goals based on evidence of success. Some of the categories in which that success is required include student achievement, staff competency and effectiveness, and accountability for use of federal funds. Thus, with emphasis on systemic accountability in those categories, education leaders will need to understand that practicing new concepts of organizational leadership is essential. Those concepts include understanding that leadership is a behavioral science and knowing (and educating teachers about) the fundamental theories of leadership. Change in education moves slowly, but I believe the three points mentioned earlier are very clear and demonstrate that education leadership is about to undergo the most profound changes ever.

> We need to do just what we did when we were putting NCLB together, and that is to keep our focus on what's in the best interest of American children. How can we ensure that we educate more of America's kids and give every child a chance at a decent education? If we keep our focus on what's in the best interest of the kids, we'll make the right decisions. **(Congressman John Boehner, personal communication, May 21, 2008)**

This chapter provides a brief overview of the history of leadership theories and describes some of those theories and leadership in general. It discusses what a transformation of education leadership might look like in schools in the future, focusing on some ideas about leadership training and preparation and how leaders might empower teachers to be leaders and organize professional learning teams.

> It can be done, but it takes a lot of leadership. It takes a leader, a teacher in the classroom, a principal, a superintendent, a board of education member, or somebody who touches children and motivates them to accomplish everything they can within their capabilities. **(Congressman Howard "Buck" McKeon, personal communication, February 27, 2008)**

My intent for discussing certain aspects of a transformation of education leadership is to encourage school leaders to look at their organizations and reflect on how they could be led in new and different ways in order to be more successful in this global compliance-, results-, and accountability-driven environment. There isn't one best solution for all education settings. But clearly the traditional models of school leadership are not working well in a number of places, so it makes sense to embrace a more contemporary approach using a leader-follower mindset that empowers teachers. The problems in education have become so complex that solving them requires a systemic team approach.

Organizational leadership is defined differently in the 21st century than it was in the past. Now it is more about empowering workers, building their knowledge about work, and motivating them to continuously work to improve their organizations. The Internet has also led to a global environment that has had a profound effect on organizations and leadership. For international companies, it has led to virtual teams that, together, can work a 24-hour shift, providing instant access to critical information on important work-related topics and a transparency on leadership that requires leaders to learn new communication and behavioral skills. Every word a leader speaks, every action taken, is instantly known around the world and disseminated via Internet applications such as YouTube and Facebook. The frequent comment about local education leaders working in a fishbowl has never been more accurate. Leaders must recognize the changing times and adjust their leadership styles to function effectively in the 21st-century workplace.

HISTORY OF LEADERSHIP THEORIES

One of the seminal books on leadership was written by Bernard Bass (1990). *Bass and Stogdill's Handbook of Leadership* actually begins by discussing leaders as prophets, chiefs, and kings who served as symbols, representatives, and models for their people as far back as the Old and New Testaments. Bass and Stogdill's work on leadership demonstrates that it is a very old practice, and over thousands of years and considerable research, there is still a distinct lack of conclusive evidence that would enable someone to say, "If I did the following, I would be an effective leader." On the other hand, the research has identified practices, skills, and traits that contribute to effective leadership. As I pointed out earlier, Sharon Daloz Parks (2005) says that leadership can be learned. Thus, understanding leadership theories is important for those who aspire to be leaders. It isn't practical to ask someone to lead a group without providing some training on understanding how to be a leader. Understanding the theories will provide leaders with a toolbox of ideas that they can use in different contexts.

But first, it is important to agree on a definition of what leadership actually is. Bass (1990) says there are "almost as many different definitions of leadership as there are persons who have attempted to define the concept" (p. 11). He said that as early as 1902, the leader was always the nucleus of a tendency because all social movements would be found to consist of tendencies having such nuclei. Other theorists' leadership definitions that Bass presents include leadership as the preeminence of one or a few individuals in a group in controlling societal phenomena, the centralization of one person as an expression of power of all, and a point of polarization for group cooperation. In education, this likely explains how superintendents and principals over time have been perceived as those individuals primarily responsible for leading their districts or buildings, with very little decision-making responsibility delegated to others.

In a more recent discussion of leadership, Antonakis, Cianciolo, and Sternberg (2004) say that "leadership is a complex and diverse field of knowledge, and trying to make sense of leadership research can become an intimidating endeavor" (p. 3). They go on to say that, in principle, leadership can be defined as an influencing process and that this process is distinguished from the use of power and management. Influencing others to sincerely follow the vision of a leader takes more than simply issuing an edict through the use of power or the formal role of authority as a manager.

Additional support for the notion that leadership is a process comes from Hughes, Ginnett, and Curphy (2006), who define leadership as "the process of influencing an organized group toward accomplishing its goals" (p. 8). It involves something happening as a result of the interaction between a leader and followers. They also emphasize that leadership and management are very different. They quote Hellriegel, Slocum, and Woodman as saying that

> a manager is a person who directs the work of employees and is responsible for results. An effective manager brings a degree of order and consistency to tasks. A leader, by contrast, inspires employees with a vision and helps them cope with change. (p. 391)

By contrasting the difference between leaders and managers, Hughes et al. (2006) address an important point for 21st-century education leadership. The difference between leadership and management is a topic that has been discussed by many leadership writers. The distinction is clear, and today's school leaders need to influence their stakeholders to buy in to their visions for school improvement initiatives. Thus, it is important to recognize that leadership is a process of influence and not simply one person using power to compel others to do what they are asked to do.

Finally, Daft (2008) supports the concept that leadership is about influencing others to come together around a common vision. He says that leadership involves the following:

- personal responsibility and integrity
- change
- shared purpose
- followers
- influence
- intention

These key points about what leadership involves are informative for school leaders. Accepting personal responsibility is important for all educators who are leading a project. Integrity is a personal characteristic that has received considerable attention lately, particularly with business leaders whose moral compass led them to lose sight of the fact that people placed great trust in them. Followers lost a lot of their financial security because of egregious leadership behavior that lacked integrity.

Most leadership work today involves change. Understanding the process of how to lead change is essential for successful school improvement initiatives. In their book *The Heart of Change*, John Kotter and Dan Cohen (2002) provide a good eight-step model for leading change:

- Increase urgency.
- Build the guiding team.
- Get the vision right.
- Communicate for buy-in.
- Empower action.
- Create short-term wins.
- Don't let up.
- Make change stick.

Now let's return to Daft's (2008) final four elements of leadership: shared purpose, followers, influence, and intention. Since contemporary thinking about leadership focuses on it as a process of influencing others, leaders must create a shared purpose for their followers. Which brings us to the next point: if one is going to lead, then there need to be followers. And gaining followers and creating a shared purpose will require the ability to influence the group to buy in to the leadership vision. Finally, it has to be the intent of the leader and followers to accept responsibility for the ultimate success of their undertaking.

It would seem logical to conclude that an acceptable definition of leadership is that it is a process of influencing others to collectively follow with sincere commitment a vision that will achieve results. The process is collaborative and empowering to all who are involved, and a team mindset keeps everyone equally engaged in the process.

One premise of this book is that teachers must be part of the leadership team in schools. This premise incorporates the notion that they have the power and authority to do what they are asked without becoming mired down in an overwhelming burden of bureaucratic rules and procedures. The role that teachers will be given necessitates that they receive the appropriate leadership training to do the work. It is generally safe to assume that when teachers are asked to lead education projects, they are expected to do it based on their experience and not whether they have had any training in leadership.

School leaders have traditionally emerged from higher education programs that prepared them for their leadership positions, programs that often include courses that are more about education administration than the science and theory of leadership. It isn't unusual to hear school administrators say that they never had training for the experiences they are going through in their roles as school leaders.

As the challenges and responsibilities for education leaders grow more complex, it should be emphatically understood that knowledge of leadership theories is essential if they are to be equipped with a variety of strategies to deal with different situations. Leaders need to understand the complexity of organizations, the environments in which they operate, and the relationship between their work and the needs of their followers.

> Leaders need different kinds of training, and the more we can provide for improving the quality of education will be helpful. One thing I have seen as a school board member is that the work in schools is between the administration and teachers, so I wish we could get over that by working together; this is not the role of the federal government. **(Congresswoman Judy Biggert, personal communication, August 7, 2007)**

Daft (2008) posits that leadership has changed over time. He discusses the evolution of leadership theory in terms of six basic categories, and much of the writing on this topic follows essentially the same categories:

- great man
- trait
- behavior
- contingency
- influence
- relational

The great man theory is probably the one most people associate with leadership. When asked who was a great leader, people commonly respond with Abraham Lincoln, Mahatma Gandhi, Eleanor Roosevelt, Winston Churchill, Rosa Parks, or some other individual who has a reputation as someone who accomplished great things. The individual was perceived as the leader and the reason for successful achievement. The great man theory basically evolved around men as leaders who were born with leadership qualities that enabled them to wield control and power over people in order to accomplish things. One of the classic great man images is George C. Scott's portrayal of General George Patton in the movie *Patton*. Scott appears before a screen filled with the American flag as background and offers an intimidating portrait of a military leader. It is an excellent metaphor for the great man theory.

Around 1920, researchers moved away from the great man theory and began to look at the traits and characteristics that distinguished leaders from their followers. The trait theory relied on the belief that those who led were different from those who followed, and because of those differences it would be possible to identify potential leaders. Researchers looked for traits and characteristics possessed by leaders. Stogdill (1948) reported that intelligence, alertness, insight, responsibility, initiative, persistence, self-confidence, and sociability were leadership traits. Mann (1959, cited in Bass, 1990) added masculinity, adjustment, dominance, extroversion, and conservatism. Stogdill (1974) later added achievement, persistence, insight, cooperativeness, tolerance, and influence to the list. Then Kirkpatrick and Locke (1991) added drive, motivation, integrity, cognitive ability, and task knowledge to the list of positive attributes for leaders to possess.

Although research on trait theory fell somewhat out of favor in the early 1990s, it has recently emerged as an important consideration to identify potentially effective leaders. The 2008 presidential campaign between Barack Obama and John McCain consistently resulted in debate over which candidate had the best leadership qualities. Despite the different traits possessed by the candidates, each was considered a leader by his followers.

By the early 1950s, there was a new emphasis on what leaders do rather than on their personalities. Researchers focused on behavior theory, which offered the opportunity to observe leaders and what they do rather than try to attribute their success to personal characteristics. The characteristics and traits of leaders were actually thought to be the basis for manifesting their behavioral skills and competencies. Behavior theorists observed a number of behaviors in leaders to determine which ones led to effective leadership. Although there is no conclusive evidence that any one behavior will lead to being a successful leader, some of the following are behaviors found in such leaders:

- has good communication skills
- demonstrates commitment
- is adaptable
- creates a motivational environment
- is efficient
- focuses on results
- establishes plans
- builds relationships
- develops oneself
- analyzes problems
- is a strategic systems thinker
- fosters teamwork
- innovates
- manages conflict (Hughes et al., 2006, p. 208)

This partial list of leadership behaviors is a good example of the many competencies effective leaders must exhibit. These skills can be both learned and refined, and school leaders should be given sufficient training to make them part of their daily routines.

Some of the most important behavioral leadership studies were completed at The Ohio State University and the University of Michigan. The Ohio State studies measured different leader behavior in work settings, and the University of Michigan studies were designed to learn about leadership behavior and its impact on employee performance (Northouse, 2009). Simply stated, the researchers were attempting to determine whether leaders focused on organizational goals or the needs of their employees. A number of leadership theories emerged from these behavioral studies, but for purposes of this book, I focus on whether they are organizationally goal driven, employee centered, or somewhere between the two.

The implications of behavioral theory for education, in terms of compliance in a standards-based accountability environment, concern balancing the needs of the organization with the needs of the employees. Education leaders are under considerable pressure to produce results in schools that are confronted with complex challenges while being responsive to employees who are often protected by laws and collective bargaining contracts that necessitate cooperation to achieve the intended results. Understanding behavioral theories can help leaders adopt the balanced leadership style that is needed in a 21st-century education organization.

Contingency theory, also known as situational leadership, deals with the situation in which leadership actually occurs. It identifies leadership effectiveness with the situation and assumes that the effectiveness of the leader's behavior is contingent on organizational situations (Daft, 2008). There are a number of situations that arise in which those who emerge as leaders were the least expected to do so. Yet time and time again, people unexpectedly become leaders because of their own personal characteristics and the situation. How many people who had not previously been seen as leaders led in the World Trade Centers on September 11, 2001? Were there secretaries, custodians, and other nonmanagerial workers who gathered groups of followers and made courageous decisions? In many of the unthinkable school shooting tragedies, were there teachers and others who were not the formal school leaders who nonetheless took control of the situation and maintained as much order as possible?

There are several strengths and weaknesses of the contingency theory, according to Northouse (2009):

Strengths

- It is supported by empirical research.
- It broadens understanding of leadership by considering the impact of situations.

- It is predictive and informs what type of leadership is likely to be effective in specific situations.
- It doesn't require that people be effective leaders in all situations.
- Personal assessment data about the leader enable people to develop leadership profiles for their organizations.

Weaknesses

- It fails to explain why some leadership styles are more effective in some situations and not others.
- The scale/instrument used to measure leadership effectiveness is not considered a valid instrument.
- It fails to explain what organizations should do when there is a mismatch between the leader and the situation in which the leader works.

There are strengths and weaknesses in all of the leadership theories, but Northouse (2009) cautions those who support the contingency theory to use it with an understanding of both the good and the bad. Clearly, having the ability to determine how a leader will react to a certain situation would provide important information to those making decisions about who should lead. A case can certainly be made for the need to match the formal leaders of school districts and buildings with the contextual situations in which they will be expected to lead.

The influence theory of leadership is probably one of the most important theories for today's education leaders. It examines the processes between leaders and followers. Daft (2008) discusses charismatic leadership as the type of leadership influence that is not based on position or formal authority. As I mentioned earlier, the 2008 presidential election focused on leadership qualities. Barack Obama had the unusual capacity to draw extremely large crowds to campaign rallies, which prompted a number of people to write about his charisma and how it influenced followers to buy in to his vision for America. Charismatic leaders can also use their charisma to influence followers for negative purposes. One such leader was Jim Jones, who took his followers out of the United States and persuaded them to commit mass suicide. So it is clear that leadership influence can have both positive and negative attributes. What is most important to understand is that influential leaders have the unique capacity to inspire their followers to accept their vision.

Influence theory incorporates the concept of transformational leadership rather than transactional leadership. Daft (2008) cites four differences between the two:

- Transformational leaders develop followers into leaders.
- Transformational leaders elevate the concerns of followers from lower-level needs to higher-level needs. (In Maslow's hierarchy, lower-level needs are physical and higher-level needs are about self-actualization.)

- Transformational leaders inspire followers to go beyond their own interests to those for the good of the group.
- Transformational leaders offer a vision for the future and articulate it in a way that makes the pain of change worth the effort.

Transactional leaders accomplish their goals more often by using the carrot-and-stick approach. They determine what the followers need and then offer to meet those needs in exchange for the followers meeting the goals of the organization. Transformational leaders, on the other hand, use their influence to achieve organizational goals. They use their vision, shared values, and beliefs to build relationships with employees, creating a mutual relationship of respect that results in achieving organizational goals. Bill George (2007) offers this description of a transformational leader in his book *True North:*

> Just as a compass points toward a magnetic pole, your true north pulls you toward the purpose of your leadership. When you follow your internal compass, your leadership will be authentic, and people will naturally want to associate with you. Although others may guide or influence you, your truth is derived from your life story, and only you can determine what it should be. (p. xxiii)

Transformational leadership is the best model for 21st-century business and education, but it is also one that takes the most effort and requires sincere leadership. It should be understood, however, that balancing the sincerity of leadership with the pressures of compliance and the need to innovate is a relatively new phenomenon for education leadership. Doing so will necessitate new leadership strategies in schools and improved leadership training. (These topics will be covered later in this chapter.)

The final theory of leadership is relational theory, and it is also quite important to today's education leaders. Relational theory focuses on the relationship between the leader and followers and how they interact and influence one another. This theory also incorporates transformational leadership, as discussed in the previous description of influence theory, and servant leadership.

The concept of servant leadership was introduced by Robert Greenleaf in 1970. Essentially, servant leadership is about leaders being more concerned with the needs of their followers than their own needs. Further, servant leaders empathize with their followers, taking care to nurture them (Northouse, 2009). Greenleaf believed that leadership is bestowed on a person who is by nature a servant. Servant leadership theory is different from the other types of leadership and elicits a very different discussion about the relationship between leaders and followers. For some, the notion that the leader is a servant to the followers is contrary to what most people believe are the underlying principles of the leadership process.

Influence and relational theories have the most significant application for education leaders in today's schools. Almost everyone who is talking about transforming schools emphasizes the importance of teamwork and committing to a clear and shared organizational vision. Influence and relational are the most difficult leadership styles to use, and they present complex organizational challenges when attempting to achieve success in a compliance environment. Nonetheless, leadership that lacks a good relationship with followers is not likely to produce long-term, sustained results. It is critically important for leaders to work diligently to establish good working relationships with their colleagues.

SUMMARY

This section on leadership theories is a very brief overview of how they evolved over time. It is apparent that the early thinking was that leaders were great men who singularly achieved their accomplishments. Subsequently, theorists began looking at the traits of effective leaders. Were there certain qualities that distinguished them from other people, such as confidence, extrovert personalities, and superior intelligence? Then theorists began studying leader behaviors to see if leaders acted in a way that distinguished them from others. The next stage of leadership theory analyzed the situation to determine if different acts of leadership were used in different situations. Ultimately, contemporary researchers have come to focus on the relationship between leaders and followers and the influence that leaders have.

Warren Bennis (2007) makes an important point about contemporary leadership vividly clear: "Psychologists have not sorted out which traits define leaders or whether leadership exists outside of specific situations, and yet we know with absolute certainty that a handful of people have changed millions of lives and reshaped the world" (p. 2). Bennis goes on to say,

> I often show a slide that includes dozens of names, from Sitting Bull and Susan B. Anthony to Kofi Annan and Carly Fiorina, and I ask the audience what these leaders have in common. In fact, the single commonality among these men and women is that all of them have or had willing followers. (p. 3)

The body of literature on leadership is voluminous. Just go to any bookstore and wander into the section containing books on leadership. It is filled with numerous books that discuss the topic from just about any perspective imaginable. I have written this brief overview of theories to provide a context for understanding the concepts of leadership, but I have barely scratched the surface. It is important for those who are expected to lead to have the proper background and training in order to have every chance of succeeding, and there is so much more that could be said on the topic of leadership, but hopefully this overview will enable you to discuss the type that will be effective in your setting. When embarking on leading school improvement work and innovation initiatives, it is worthwhile to note a comment from Keith Grint (2005): "It only requires the good follower to do nothing for leadership to fail" (p. 133).

> As we design our professional development program for education leaders, our approach is to translate research into some kind of guidance to train people to have the knowledge and skills to lead. We use taxonomy to organize our work. If I were going to advise a superintendent or principal, I use the taxonomy to be clear on what is it from our work and others' that leaders do that impacts the outcomes you are after (e.g., student achievement). We call that declarative knowledge, and there are four types of knowledge we discuss. First is, what is it you need to know? Then procedural knowledge: how do you transcend the idea to practice? Third, there is experiential knowledge: is what you are doing important, not only what you are doing and how you are doing it but the reasons you are doing it? Finally, there is contextual knowledge: when would you apply all of that in your context? The four types of knowledge cover the what, why, when, and how. A new superintendent or principal ought to be really clear on them. **(Tim Waters, personal communication, August 10, 2009)**

A TRANSFORMATION OF EDUCATION LEADERSHIP

> We need strong leadership at the federal, state, and school board levels as well as in the schools. Leaders need to have high expectations for their stakeholders. **(Congressman Rush Holt, personal communication, May 8, 2008)**

A tipping point for education leadership has been reached. The three points mentioned earlier, which I repeat here, create a context for the future of results-based leadership and accountability for the use of federal funding:

- Nontraditional school leaders are being appointed to lead large, urban school systems, and Secretary Duncan is calling on mayors rather than traditional superintendents to assume control of underachieving city districts.
- Increased scrutiny of monitoring and accountability for results are accompanying ARRA funding and NCLB provisions.
- The federal government was active in removing the CEO of General Motors because it didn't believe he could successfully turn the company around.

These three points combined could certainly be a prelude to the way the federal government might respond to leaders in school districts that receive federal funds who don't produce satisfactory results in the future. It is unlikely that Congress and the Department of Education are going to have much patience for not observing quick improvement in student achievement after the substantial increase in education funding in 2009. Transformation is hard work. The lead role in education transformation will be the responsibility of school superintendents, CEOs, or whatever title is used by the people in charge.

In 2009 the American Association of School Administrators invited superintendents of the year to participate in a three-day forum on transforming schools. The strategies used by these superintendents support the need to rethink the process and model of leadership in schools. They provide a foundation for making bold changes that might produce improvements that heretofore were thought not possible:

- Develop a vision and clear direction.
- Determine what students should know and be able to do.
- Use data to confront the truth about student achievement, and then talk about it.
- Create a sense of urgency.
- Think of principals as instructional leaders rather than managers.
- Know that principals cannot do it all; each principal needs a team.
- Train employees, and give them resources and time.
- Tolerate mistakes.
- Focus on transforming education instead of minor tweaking.
- Know that secondary education is the most difficult to change.
- Have patience. (p.10)

Offered as recommendations, these strategies not only support a new mindset for leading schools but are also aligned with the more contemporary leadership theories that view teamwork as an essential ingredient in the process.

School leaders are under considerable pressure to quickly produce improved results under NCLB and ARRA. There is a distinct need to implement different models of leadership in schools in order to have a better chance to be successful achieving those results. As Wilfred Drath says,

leadership has become more difficult because of challenges that are not just complicated but also unpredictable. Such challenges demand that people and organizations fundamentally change, and make it virtually impossible for an individual leader to accomplish the work of leadership. What is needed is a more inclusive and collective leadership, a prospect that although difficult to achieve holds much potential. (quoted in Munro, 2008, p. 29)

Drath emphasizes that no matter how skilled the leader, complex challenges preclude any leader from doing it alone; a whole system and all of the people in that system need to address those challenges together.

To change the traditional model of leadership in schools, it will be necessary to use new training programs for education leaders. This will involve rethinking the required coursework in preparation programs in universities and the ongoing professional development activities for current practitioners. Another important part of a different leadership model is the need to recognize the leadership contributions that could be made by teachers. Delegating leadership to teachers who have the authority to make decisions will not be an easy transition in schools that have relied on the more traditional superintendent/principal decision-making process.

> If the principal is the only person doing the leadership and says, "This is what is going to happen and here is why," teachers still have to buy into that. Teachers still are the ones who actually make it happen. So what we would rather see happen is for teachers to say, "What is going on in my classroom and my colleagues' classrooms isn't working," and see that bubble up from the people who have the prolonged contact with children. **(Jennifer Fisler, personal communication, April 15, 2009)**

There is also evidence that Generation Y teachers, those who were born after 1977, have a different perspective on how schools should be run. As these new teachers begin to replace the large number of Baby Boomer teachers who are retiring, the implications for leaders who are recruiting and attempting to retain new teachers will have to be recognized. It will be important to create learning teams that focus on substantive improvement issues by building knowledge and innovation and not simply the process of forming the teams. Gen Y teachers want to be inspired in their work. The learning team will help meet their needs.

TRAINING PROGRAMS FOR SCHOOL LEADERS

Preparing School Leaders for a Changing World

In this report commissioned by the Wallace Foundation, M. Christine DeVita, president of the foundation, said in a letter introducing the report:

> Study after study has shown that the training principals typically receive in university programs and from their own districts doesn't do nearly enough to prepare them for their roles as leaders of learning. A staggering 80 percent of superintendents and 69 percent of

principals think that leadership training in schools of education is out of touch with the realities of today's districts, according to a recent Public Agenda survey. (Darling-Hammond, LaPointe, Meyerson, Orr, & Cohen, 2007)

If there were any more evidence or reason to consider the need to transform education leadership for the 21st century, it would seem DeVita's comments say it all. *Preparing School Leaders for a Changing World* reviews eight exemplary pre- and inservice principal development programs and presents these findings:

- Exemplary pre- and inservice programs share many common features.
- These programs produce well-prepared leaders who engage in effective practices.
- Program success is influenced by leadership, partnerships, and financial support.
- Funding strategies influence the design and effectiveness of programs.

The lessons learned are important if the real goal is to change the mindset of those who are expected to lead schools and achieve success in this new compliance environment. Participants in these successful programs identified several factors as critical to their success: a comprehensive and coherent curriculum, a curriculum that emphasizes instructional leadership and school improvement, social and professional support for their cohort, and well-designed internships.

National Institute for School Leadership

What we found when we began to put this leadership program together and to do the research on it was that professions such as medicine, law, the military, and business were intensely focused on past practices, on their own practices, and on lessons learned. We didn't find quite the same emphasis on the practices surrounding teaching, learning, or leadership in the education profession. Many educators were, in my view anyway, less reflective on and attentive to the description, dissemination, and refinement of the best instructional practices. The second main insight from a look at other professions was that leadership training needed to be cohort-based, where, for example, principals could share and benchmark best practices in instructional leadership. Research clearly tells us the way we are going to foster higher achievement and produce significant gains in student work is through improved instructional and leadership practices. Those were the guiding insights when we built the program. **(Robert Hughes, personal communication, March 9, 2009, on a program developed by the National Institute for School Leadership)**

The National Institute for School Leadership (NISL) offers a different approach to training school principals. It even markets the program as an executive development program. The NISL curriculum incorporates research-based leadership practices from the military, business, medicine, law, and engineering. Participants spend 27 days in class over a 15- to 18-month period and engage in online activities, face-to-face instruction, case studies, computer-assisted simulations, video presentations, and facilitated group discussions with school leaders (see www.nisl.net). NISL's mission is to develop school leaders who will drive their schools to high performance and to build district and state capacity to leverage and sustain instructional improvement. These are the components of the NISL curriculum:

- World-class vision and goals
  - o the education challenge
  - o principal as strategic thinker
  - o standards-based instructional systems and school design
  - o foundations of effective learning

- Focus on teaching and learning
  - o leadership for excellence in literacy
  - o leadership for excellence in mathematics
  - o leadership for excellence in science
  - o promoting professional learning and Phase I simulation

- Developing capacity and commitment
  - o principal as instructional leader and team builder
  - o principal as ethical leader

- Driving for results
  - o principal as driver of change
  - o culminating simulation

An impressive list of funders supported the development of NISL's program, including the Carnegie Corporation of New York, New Schools Venture Fund, the Stupski Foundation, and the Broad Foundation. What makes the program so different is that it focuses on the science of leadership yet incorporates the important aspects of instructional leadership for school principals in the curriculum. Principals going through NISL's training have the advantage of learning how leaders in other professions have achieved success and then being able to apply what they learned in their own educational context. The Broad Foundation evaluated the program and reported positive results, and participants have indicated a high level of satisfaction with their participation in the program.

One aspect of NISL's training merits special mention in this discussion of the transformation of leadership in schools: the use of case studies to help prepare education leaders for a variety of situations. Traditionally, school administrators obtained their certification to be principals and superintendents by earning degrees in higher education programs, and these programs often include a number of classes that many graduates say didn't prepare them well for their jobs. I bring this up not to be overly critical of this area of higher education but rather to call for a review of what needs to be changed in order to help leaders function more effectively in a 21st-century education environment that is more political, more diverse, and more focused on appropriate use of data and the need for real problem-solving skills.

> When I got to Fairfax County [Virginia], I realized it was a very different job and I had to be more of a politician, more of a public spokesperson. I had to be able to deal with the assortment of interest groups in the community, not the least of which were the business community, the parent community, the labor groups. With all of these things combined, I can honestly say I don't recall that I ever received in my traditional education training the preparation I needed to do that kind of job. **(Dan Domenech, personal communication, April 22, 2009)**

New York City Leadership Academy

New York City is attempting to change the way it trains principals by creating a nonprofit organization that is independent of the school system and modeled after successful private sector initiatives. The program is deeply rooted in practice. The participants are aspiring principals who are selected through a screening process, and they go through a 14-month curriculum that includes summer school and a 10-month residency overseen by a mentor who is a practicing principal. The program concludes with a summer planning session that helps participants assume a principalship in their own schools.

One aspect of this program that is especially worth noting is that participants work in teams to solve the problems of a simulated school. The leadership strategies involved in this activity are part of what new school leaders must replicate in their own settings to respond successfully to the challenges of compliance, leadership, and innovation (L. Olson, 2007).

Case Study Activity

Case study is a good learning opportunity to help school leaders investigate actual situations and apply their problem-solving abilities to an authentic situation. Yet the field of education has not often used case study work as the basis for professional development or classes for school leaders. The Harvard School of Business, however, is well known for its use of case studies in its master's degree program. In 2008 I attended a training session for education instructors at Harvard, which focused on using a new case study book for education, *Managing School Districts for High Performance* (Childress, Elmore, Grossman, & Johnson, 2007).

One advantage of using case studies is that they provide participants with an opportunity to discuss their understanding of how leadership theory applies to the situation they are addressing. The case is a replication of something that actually occurred elsewhere, and participants can learn how the situation was handled but also offer their own thoughts about how they believe it could have been handled better.

Another advantage of case study analysis is that the instructor or facilitator isn't lecturing the participants but instead is facilitating a lively discussion that actively involves them. The discussion is often the basis for numerous disagreements which enable the participants to learn more as a result of listening to everyone's thoughts about the problem and possible solutions.

The Harvard case study book covers a variety of topics and is divided into modules that include case studies on topics such as supporting personnel, building a high-performance organization, managing schools across differences, and supporting high performance over time.

The NISL program and the Harvard case study method are two important approaches to the ongoing training and preparation of school leaders. They break from traditional training content and incorporate the science of leadership and application of theory to actual problem solving using authentic situations. Congressman and Chairman of the House Committee on Education and Labor George Miller talked about the challenges of leadership, particularly with diverse groups of followers in conjunction with the leadership role of the Speaker of the House. His comments offer insight on how important it is for school leaders who are working in similarly diverse settings to use collaborative strategies. Case study analysis can enhance learning about dealing with diverse groups.

An example of leadership in this institution would be the Speaker of the House. The Speaker has the vision of where she thinks the party and caucus should go and what we should try to do for the nation—health care, education, whatever the agenda is. Every two years you get a new group of representatives; you constantly have to be talking and listening and working and giving people responsibility—giving them challenges, testing them to see what they can and can't do. You constantly have to pair up people; you might find some people work better as blue dogs, in the Black or Asian caucus. You constantly tease out the potential and the contribution they are going to make so that, at the end of the day, they carry out the vision and get the 218 votes, a majority of support in the House. I think school in many ways is not set up for that vision of leadership. **(Congressman George Miller, personal communication, May 1, 2008)**

As more emphasis is being placed on improving education leadership, the use of newer learning strategies and subject content is critically important. Not only is the current traditional leadership training process becoming outdated, but education leaders now need to take into account the differences between leading Gen Y teachers and those born in earlier generations.

Leading Gen Y Teachers

The National Comprehensive Center for Teacher Quality (TQ Center) at Learning Point Associates has reviewed the need for new strategies that school leaders must use to lead Gen Y teachers (Behrstock & Clifford, 2009). Understanding Gen Y teachers is important because the Baby Boomers, born between 1946 and 1964, are retiring and the new generation of teachers has a different perspective on how they want the workplace to operate. There are significant implications for school leaders who will have to oversee Gen Y staff. Meeting the needs of this group of teachers will help sustain the needed transformation of education leadership.

After reviewing private sector practices with Gen Y employees, the TQ Center learned that methods of recruiting and retaining these employees need to be changed. Behrstock and Clifford (2009) suggest 10 strategies for leaders to use in doing so:

- Establish a shared vision, and set goals.
- Encourage shared leadership.
- Create a positive and supportive school culture.
- Select and assign teachers effectively.
- Improve teachers' skills, knowledge, and capabilities.
- Adopt effective tools for teacher evaluation.
- Use time effectively.
- Use data effectively.
- Ensure that school facilities are adequate and functional.
- Provide effective instructional leadership.

Most if not all of these recommendations appear intuitive for school leaders, and a growing body of literature supports the need to treat Gen Y employees differently than teachers were treated in the past.

The Future for Education Leaders

The KnowledgeWorks Foundation (n.d.) has produced a complex forecast for the future of education that is highly informative for leaders in the field. It highlights key forces of change that will shape learning over the next decade and emphasizes that, in a changing world, creation and innovation are becoming more essential for success than ever before. The report's depiction of the future of education for the year 2020 contains six drivers of change, which are the forces of transformation that will remake learning. The forecast states that "over the next decade, the most vibrant innovations in education will take place outside traditional institutions" (para. 1). For leadership, it predicts that one of the trends will be open leadership and sociability. The notion is that the workplace will have open collaborative platforms that enable networked teams to self-organize and support ad hoc leaders (see www.kwfdn.org).

KnowledgeWorks believes that the technologies of cooperation remake organizational models through the way they are used by employees. The technologies enable social networks in the workplace, provide incredible amounts of readily accessible information, make transparency in the workplace possible, and ultimately change the way workers learn and interact with each other.

It would be easy to think that these predictions are way beyond the capacity of schools and that leaders can just ignore them. But the proliferation of online schools, online professional development programs, and instant communication through social networking sites such as Twitter and Facebook all present trends that are probably destined to become part of the changing school landscape.

The transformation of education leadership will require leaders who understand the implications of a digital society and the impact it will have on K–12 and higher education. Ignoring those trends might be analogous to the manner in which American auto manufacturers failed to recognize what their overseas counterparts were doing. Even though it took a long time for the trends to have a devastating effect on the American companies, the simple fact is that they may never recover and could ultimately go out of business. Hopefully, America's education leaders will take the emerging trends seriously and transform the profession in ways that will make every learner successful and prepared to participate in a globally competitive society.

Teacher Leadership

The idea was born out of a meeting we had with an expert on differentiated instruction for special education students. We began discussing how we could differentiate at the other end by thinking how we at the college level look at our students. We said that we have some students here who have the potential to be exemplary classroom teachers and who have the personal and professional skills to respectfully challenge the status quo and actually do something about that challenge. We thought about what we are doing for them. So that is how we began the teacher leadership seminar for our students. **(Jennifer Fisler, personal communication, April 15, 2009, on why we need teacher leadership and what Messiah College is doing about it)**

The education literature is filled with stories about teachers as leaders. But what is said and what is done are very different. For the most part, formal education leaders, principals and superintendents, have been required to earn advanced degrees with graduate classes in education administration and leadership. I would argue that that there is a need for formal leadership training for teachers, with emphasis on the critical components of the science of leadership. To advance the more contemporary thinking on teacher leadership, teachers must be given sufficient training on the role of leaders.

There is currently not enough emphasis on leadership training for teachers, particularly for those who are being asked to accept leadership roles. If we want teachers to be leaders, then they need opportunities to be properly prepared for their assignments. They need leadership training programs or locally planned professional development opportunities focusing on leadership. It is simply unfair and naïve to believe that asking a teacher to assume a leadership role without offering some basic training for that role will lead to positive outcomes.

Chapter 3 is about innovation and calls for teachers to be leaders and facilitators of innovation teams. That work will require them to understand the role of leaders and the concept of innovation, which is not something they can do effectively without the proper training and support.

Most of the time, teacher leaders are not really leaders but by definition administrators. They are rarely empowered to significantly change the way schools operate. The most common leadership responsibilities for teachers are as grade-level leaders in elementary schools and department chairs in high schools. Yet these roles don't generally give them a real say in the school's formal decision making beyond their small sphere of influence.

> I think teachers have to be leaders if they are going to be involved in planning instruction. If they are going to be held accountable, then they also have to have some of the authority and the skill sets to lead others. **(Chuck Morris, personal communication, April 22, 2009)**

Leadership for Student Learning (2001), a report from the Task Force on Teacher Leadership from the Institute for Educational Leadership, makes the following statement:

> We are loath as a nation to consider whether our roughly 2.78 million public school teachers should have any consequential role in schooling beyond that of closely controlled human mechanisms for funneling information into schoolchildren—and then getting out of the way. The infinite potential the nation's teachers possess for sharing their hard-earned knowledge and wisdom with players in education's decision-making circles—or even for becoming part of these circles—remains largely unexploited. (p. 1)

The report lists these basic duties that have traditionally been identified with teacher leadership:

- choosing textbooks and instructional materials
- shaping the curriculum
- setting standards for student behavior
- deciding whether students are tracked into special classes
- designing staff development and inservice programs
- setting promotion and retention policies
- deciding school budgets
- evaluating teacher performance
- selecting new teachers
- selecting new administrators (p. 3)

None of these duties would be considered real leadership responsibilities in a 21st-century organizational context. The concept of teachers as leaders and facilitators (discussed in detail in Chapter 3) is contingent on the teachers having the authority to lead a team and develop bold, new concepts that address the most serious problems in the school. Only through innovative thinking will years of failing to getting satisfactory results bring about the type of changes that are needed. That type of teacher leadership requires an understanding of using transformational-relationship strategies to work with colleagues in a leader-follower relationship. It is about giving teachers a substantive role in schools and not merely the more administrative assignments cited earlier.

So what can superintendents do to empower teachers to serve on leadership teams and accept responsibility for participating in the decision-making process? Clearly there is a caveat to teacher leadership that must overcome collective bargaining agreements when the provisions might preclude them from participating. But even collective bargaining agreements in the private sector are adapting to the more contemporary workplace environment. Many unions and management personnel have had to review how they operated in the past and make a number of compromises to survive in a globally competitive business environment.

The TQ Center offers these suggestions for implementing teacher leadership in schools:

- Value and respect the role and work of teacher leaders.
- Embrace change and allow data-driven, research-based risk taking.
- Provide affirmation for teachers' leadership tasks.
- Promote and facilitate collaboration.
- Provide technical support for teacher leaders.
- Empower teachers in their leadership tasks.
- Involve faculty in decision making. (National Comprehensive Center for Teacher Quality, 2007, p. 5)

The TQ Center also says to be careful not to do the following:

- Withhold, control, or limit power from teachers who are involved in decision making appropriate to their experience, knowledge, and expertise.
- Devalue the work and efforts made by teacher leaders.
- Place teachers in isolated rather than in collaborative situations.
- Focus on micromanaging the details instead of providing the big picture and supporting the larger goal. (National Comprehensive Center for Teacher Quality, 2007, p. 5)

From preservice teachers who are participating in the teacher leadership seminar at Messiah College to the harsh comments in the Institute of Education Leadership Task Force Report to the recommendations of the TQ Center, it is apparent that much more can and should be done to promote real leadership opportunities for teachers in schools.

Professional Learning Teams

The final topic to discuss in terms of the transformation of education leadership is professional learning teams, which can make significant contributions to the success of an organization. We operate in a knowledge- and information-focused society, so the task of these teams is to ensure that organizational knowledge is continuously being updated. Teams require leaders, and professional learning teams in schools can be ideally led by teachers. But it is important to recognize that the teams must focus on building knowledge and not on the process of team formation. That task belongs to the team leader, and that leader should have the proper training, resources, and authority to lead the team.

> It is clear that any change in a school must be accepted, appreciated and nurtured by the principal. In the case of professional learning communities, accepting, appreciating and nurturing change may be a difficult challenge for some principals, because one of the defining characteristics of professional learning communities is that power, authority and decision making are shared and encouraged. (Hord & Sommers, 2008, p. 10)

The concept of learning teams is not really new. Peter Senge (2000) discusses learning organizations in *Schools That Learn*: "It is becoming clear that schools can be re-created, made vital, and sustainably renewed not by fiat or command, and not by regulation, but by taking a learning orientation" (p. 5). One wonders why, after nearly 10 years, this notion proposed by Senge is still not a common practice in schools.

Today's organizations are most effective when focusing more on team-work and less on bureaucracy. Leading teams effectively requires training. Giving team leaders the knowledge and skills to further the organization's goals is not only sensible, but essential.

The problems educators are dealing with have become more complex. The focus on accountability with specific benchmarks defined by data can best be addressed through a team approach. The current thinking about leadership involves leaders working collaboratively with followers who share a common vision about organizational goals. Superintendents and principals will have to focus more on systemic results. Training teacher leaders to oversee teams working on serious problems, and delegating the appropriate authority to them in order to do that work, is an important part of transforming leadership in schools.

A Wallace Foundation report called *Leading for Change* (2009) cites a key objective of Harvard's executive leadership program on teaching and learning, the objective of which is consistent with the rationale presented in this chapter concerning what it will take to transform leadership in schools:

> Individuals and teams identify and improve the leadership and teamwork skills needed throughout their organizations to success-fully manage the deep changes this work entails and to establish collaborative norms that focus all adult interactions on the work of instructional improvement. (p. 5)

Chapter 3 explores in more detail the concept of teams and teachers leading innovation teams. Innovation is being discussed more and more for education, and stimulating innovative thinking will require knowledge of the innovation process, skilled leaders who understand instructional delivery, and a willingness to think creatively in new and different ways.

SUMMARY

While there is no single formula to follow, I suggest that the following foundation is essential for becoming a successful leader:

- knowing the basic theories of leadership
- understanding the work of teams
- leading through change
- managing conflict
- engaging in interpersonal and organizational communication
- maintaining ethical behavior

This list is a core for understanding how to become an effective leader. It doesn't include other important aspects of leadership such as using research and data, strategic planning, and labor relations. Instead, it is a core of topics that all leaders need for their toolbox to personalize their perspective on leadership. But equally important is knowing yourself and your personal beliefs. In *True North,* Bill George (2007) says, "Leaders are highly complex human beings, people who have distinctive qualities that cannot be sufficiently described by lists of traits or characteristics. . . . You have to understand yourself, because the hardest person you will ever lead is yourself" (p. xxxiii).

According to Stephen Reicher, Michael Platow, and Alexander Haslam (2007), the new psychology of leadership is based on three facts, which summarize what I have said about the transformation of education leadership in the 21st century. First, effective leaders must understand the values and opinions of their followers to enable a productive dialogue with team members about what the group stands for and how it should act. Second, no fixed set of personality traits can ensure good leadership because the most desirable traits depend on the nature of the group being led. Finally, leaders must adopt a strategy not only to fit in with their group but also to shape the group's identity in a way that makes their own agenda and policies appear to be an expression of that identity.

Thus, in schools, announcing a compliance requirement might be a leadership strategy that produces results, but it won't be nearly as effective as using the strategy of influencing others in such a way that they will understand the compliance requirement is worthwhile. Implementation of NCLB by the U.S. Department of Education, for example, was based primarily on using sanctions and authority with a top-down leadership strategy. In Chapter 4, former U.S. Secretary of Education Richard Riley is quoted on the style of leadership he might have used if NCLB had been the law when he was in office. In essence, he discusses the importance of using incentives rather than sanctions to get people to comply with the challenging requirements in NCLB. Leadership is a complex process, and all leaders need a set of skills that enables them to adjust to different situations.

It depends. Compromise to the point where the objective is not reached in order to claim a political victory, no. Better to do nothing than give the appearance of reform when there is none. There is a fine line, and if you can find common ground with people who are opposed to your efforts and achieve the desired results, yes. Compromise, or whatever you want to call it, is important but not to do the opposite, which is to fail to achieve the objective. Which in our case, as it should be in every place in the country, is continued rising student achievement. If you can't achieve that, there are certain things you can't compromise—the underlying principles of the reform you are proposing as a leader. **(Former Florida Governor Jeb Bush, personal communication, July 20, 2009, on whether compromise is an essential element for initiatives to bring about change)**

DISCUSSION ACTIVITY QUESTIONS

1. Name a great leader, and explain why you selected that individual.

2. What type of leadership would be successful in your organization to motivate people to work diligently to overcome your most significant obstacles? Why?

3. Does your organization recognize the difference between its Gen Y teachers and those from other generations?

NOTE

1. Despite substantial federal funding, task force oversight, and a new CEO, on June 1, 2009, GM filed for Chapter 11 bankruptcy and would go on to receive even more federal funding to help the company survive.

3

Innovation

*If you are going to be a leader, you don't get to live in a comfort zone—
especially if you think you want to be innovative.*

—Congressman and chair of the House Committee
on Education and Labor, George Miller, May 1, 2008

INTRODUCTION

One of the most frequently heard words in education, business, and
Congress lately is *innovation*. It seems like everyone wants to be known as
an innovator, yet there is often no commonly understood definition or
even agreement as to what is meant by it. To some, the most recent complex high-tech device, such as an iPhone, is innovation, while to others it
is something as simple as a cup holder in a car. But for the future of education, it will be incredibly important to make significantly big improvements in teaching and learning and for innovation to be the cornerstone of
those improvements. There is a serious need to look at new ways of teaching and learning that align with a 21st-century world that functions with
technology and virtual reality. It simply is not logical to believe that many
of the current products, programs, and practices being used in schools will
lead to the intended outcomes for higher student achievement. That isn't
to say that many of those products, programs, and practices can't be used,
but they will have to be used in new and different ways for greater success.

So what is innovation? How can it be defined for educators working on improvement initiatives? I define innovation as a new solution to an ongoing problem that achieves substantially improved results. That solution can be a product, program, or a practice. It can be simple or complex, although I offer the caveat that most innovation conceived of in schools by educators will likely, and should, be more of the simple variety. And while there are currently some good and interesting innovations in education, the system tends to be far too decentralized to bring those innovations to every classroom, unlike the large-scale awareness and implementation of most innovations in medicine and consumer products. What is often noted as a strength for American public education—local control—in this instance is often a detriment because there are likely many good ideas incubating in the approximately 15,000 public school districts in the United States that never make their way to all of the nation's schools, yet they could potentially be effective and innovative solutions to problems that other educators are confronting.

Consider the transformation in radial keratotomy eye surgery from using a scalpel to using a laser. This innovation is readily used by almost all ophthalmologists because it is more effective and has better results. There is clear evidence and research that supports the need to use lasers rather than scalpels for this procedure. Further, medical schools prepare future eye surgeons to use lasers, thus ensuring that the practice is implemented on a large scale by almost all eye surgeons. Yet in education, there is a paucity of innovative, transformational ideas taught to students preparing to become teachers that are universally accepted and acknowledged to be effective in the contexts in which they are used.

> I am a great believer in research, but what it would take to make education research based are studies that are so arguably persuasive in terms of helping to establish as fact something that educators can't turn their back on. **(Congressman Michael Castle, personal communication, June 12, 2007, on the comparison between medical and education research)**

Congressman Castle's comment clearly supports the notion that there is a need to change the thinking about how education research can support innovation and improvement in teaching and learning. In addition, that research would need more universal acceptance by those in higher education who prepare teachers and school leaders. Far too often, these concepts end up becoming the substance of ideological debate and not the basis for building on a body of knowledge to improve them. Thus, moving innovative ideas to every classroom in the country is a daunting, if not impossible, challenge.

Consider this: consumers line up hours ahead of time to get the latest iteration of the iPhone because they want the newest and most innovative cell phone technology. They crave innovation that can enhance their daily lives. Unlike with laser eye surgery or the iPhone, educators don't tend to adopt a new idea or technological breakthrough in ways that can impact all schools. But why? Certainly there are products, programs, and practices being used in schools that have the potential to result in universally improved student learning and teaching effectiveness.

Even a good education innovation may go unnoticed by a majority of the profession despite its potentially successful impacts. Failure to use innovation on a large scale in education should not be passed off with mere complacency. Innovation is arguably going to be the most important process to transform public education in this compliance- and accountability-driven environment if it is to remain a viable public institution. There is clear evidence that the private sector is seizing an opportunity to make inroads into traditional public education activities. Some examples include the growth of private tutoring firms under No Child Left Behind (NCLB) and the rapidly expanding number of online education services. The simple fact is that without innovation, the current system of public education remains in many ways outdated and an easy target for entrepreneurs who offer parents alternatives that give their children more and better opportunities to succeed.

Innovation can be implemented through products, programs, or practices. In a presentation I gave on the topic of innovation, I discussed it as both complex and simple. For complex innovation, I showed the audience a new digital pen that can record a conversation or lecture while a student uses it to take notes. Using the digital pen enables the student to capture an audio recording of what is being said to accompany the notes. The controls for the pen are on digital paper in a notebook that comes with the pen. So, for example, if you are listening to a lecture and taking notes but can't keep up with the speaker, you touch the pen to the "record" icon on the paper and it will record the lecture from that point. This complex innovation is surprisingly easy to use and has great potential for students who are not good note takers.

For simple innovation, I talked about how easy it is to travel with a suitcase. Just imagine years ago when travelers had to actually carry their suitcases—off the ground. Then Bernard Sadow took two old ideas, wheels and a suitcase, and combined them. An incredibly simple innovation made traveling much more convenient; travelers no longer had to carry their heavy suitcases, and the luggage industry was transformed.

I also like to remind audiences that almost one hundred years ago a Norwegian named Johan Vaaler invented the paper clip. The paper clip, a very simple innovation, is still widely used today. Just think about the process Vaaler might have gone through to figure out how to hold multiple pieces of paper together.

My point is that simple ideas can have profound impacts. If we harness the collective thinking of educators, it could probably result in many innovations with the potential to transform the profession. There is a critical and compelling need for education leaders to create the conditions in schools that enable educators to work on and lead innovation teams. Using a framework that I discuss later in the chapter, these teams would identify the most serious problems facing them and use an innovation process to solve them. The end result would ideally be new ideas to solve those problems.

> It's difficult because some hard choices have to be made, and I don't think the American people or their political leaders realize yet the competition that is coming. That is something I see now running the U.S.-China Working Group. A huge employer in my congressional district, Motorola, acknowledges that the entire future of the company and all those jobs in my district depend on innovation and trends outside the United States. Very few people understand that. **(Congressman Mark Kirk, personal communication, July 25, 2007)**

Both simple and complex innovations are essential to improve teaching and learning. Many of the current products, programs, and practices are not keeping up with 21st-century educational needs, and international comparisons of U.S. student achievement indicate that the United States is not remaining competitive internationally. One only has to review the results of the Third International Mathematics and Science Study and its follow-up studies, the Program for International Student Achievement and the Program for International Reading Study, for proof of this. And while it is difficult to generalize about all U.S. students, clearly there is a wide achievement gap in the country between those who are and aren't doing well that must be narrowed. Far too many disadvantaged and rural students are not achieving at acceptable levels. Past and current educational practices have not been used with any degree of substantial success to narrow that gap.

What is critical, and of most importance for innovation, is the process that is cultivated within a school or district to come up with new solutions to problems. Innovation work is highly collaborative and incorporates new ways for groups to collaborate on problem solving, so it would not be a radical idea for schools to use "innovation coaches" to work with groups of teachers, administrators, and others trying to solve challenging problems in their schools by approaching solutions with new and different thinking and practices.

I am not suggesting that schools respond to every problem with an intense innovation process. But I do believe that prioritizing the most serious problems and focusing on new and different thinking using an innovation process can lead to successful solutions. That process will require that educators confront situations in which success has been elusive with totally different perspectives. That thinking includes a willingness to take risks, break the mold of old ideas and solutions, and resist the "buzz word" trends that permeate the profession. It also means gaining support from boards of education to do experimental work, disengage from ideology, and recognize that failure can be a learning experience.

Innovation groups in schools will have to take risks and will not always produce successful results. Sandy Speicher, from IDEO (an innovation and design company I discuss in more detail later in this chapter), points out that her company "says 'Fail early to succeed sooner.' We intentionally use the word *fail* because we know that it hits something in all of us—nobody wants to fail, but failure is a huge part of learning. When you don't succeed at something you have tried, you have to ask why" (personal communication, August 5, 2008). Learning from the innovation process will not only expand educators' knowledge about a problem, but also lead to improved products, programs, and practices for teaching and learning

As discussed earlier in this book, it is unlikely that federal and state accountability laws will be less demanding in the future. The challenges confronting education leaders and teachers will necessitate new ways of looking at how the teaching-learning process can be changed. Beyond merely solving accountability issues, innovation may be increasingly important to school leaders who have to balance budgets with limited resources. It is also unlikely that taxpayers will continue to fund a system that is so costly to operate because of the need for human capital when technology can potentially be used to reduce some of those costs. I am not suggesting that all teachers and support personnel can be eliminated, but clearly technology can play a greater role in the learning process and fewer personnel in a school district can substantially reduce operational costs.

Some human capital jobs have already been eliminated through the use of innovative technology. As much as people want to talk to a real person, one very common example of what I am suggesting is the recording you frequently get when calling businesses that have implemented innovative voice technology. Whether it is the best solution to reducing costs isn't the point. The point is that innovation must support a process of reducing costs in schools so that limited resources can be directed to the most important priorities. Reducing human capital in schools through innovative use of technology won't be easy. But if there are lessons to be learned from the financial meltdown at the end of 2008, as many businesses went bankrupt or out of business entirely, they are that economic efficiency is essential and innovative ideas are critical to moving in the right direction. Finding better ways to operate schools more efficiently and achieving greater success at lower costs is not a radical notion that should be disregarded. The lessons from the 2008 financial crisis should be a warning to educators that finding less expensive ways to operate schools while still improving student achievement is important and necessary.

It should be clear from earlier chapters in this book that compliance with federal and state laws, as unreasonable as they may appear, will be an ongoing challenge for educators. To successfully address that challenge will require effective education leadership from all segments of the profession. Teachers need to be given more responsibility leading improvement teams and the proper training to be successful in doing so. Leaders will need to use 21st-century leadership strategies that recognize the need to involve and gain acceptance from followers and create an innovative culture in their schools and districts. That is not going to be an easy task.

Finally, we are confronted with a very different environment for educating 21st-century students. Many students in today's classrooms are not familiar with some of the resources or tools their teachers are most comfortable using. For example, most students today are technologically competent and access information and communicate socially using a computer or cell phone. They access newspapers, magazines, and reports on the Internet. But most teachers are from a generation that is accustomed to doing all of this in print. The proof of this chasm is the demise or bankruptcy of so many newspapers and magazines. As Congressman Miller put it, "students are digital and schools are analog, but the schools are trying to hold on to the analog world because there is a comfort zone" (personal communication, May 1, 2008). The future will necessitate schools becoming digital and leaving that comfort zone.

If schools are going to be innovative, it will require a new way of looking at how their staff views problems and solutions. I have long believed that one reason for not having much innovation in schools is the failure to provide the proper conditions for people to participate in innovation activities. I look back with pride to the board of education I worked for in West Northfield District 31 in Illinois, when it approved approximately $25,000 to work with on a project called World Scan. The project involved using a computer, laser disc, CD, and videotape in conjunction with each other. This was in 1989, so it was the cutting edge of merging technologies at the time. There were no guarantees it would work, but the board saw value in the opportunity for the teachers to work with IBM staff, other vendors, and the newest technology at the time. Today we don't give a thought to using those technologies built in to computers, but at the time, it was a truly innovative and cutting-edge project for educators.

Education leaders need to take a new look at how professional development is provided and the type of organizational culture needed to break the traditional mold of how things are done. They need to find the proper balance between what has worked and what needs to be changed. That means focusing on new ways of communicating with staff, creating social networks that extend beyond school or district boundaries, and convincing policymakers that more funds are needed in order to have an impact on the fundamental problems confronting educators. Even though I have said that economic efficiency is needed in schools, I want to be clear that there is still a need for policymakers, particularly at the federal level, to increase the investment in promoting a knowledge culture that produces innovation for schools.

THE INNOVATION PROCESS

Let me be very clear about one point: In this overview of innovative thinking and how it has been used in businesses, I am not touting business innovation as the only way for educators to be innovative. But the simple fact is that many successful businesses have gone through an innovation cycle, and educators can use what has been learned in business as a basis for thinking about how to innovate in their schools and districts.

> That's talking about what you would like to do versus political realities and things that can be accomplished. It's hard to be an innovator at the federal level. I think you can be an innovator in the classroom, in a school district, even the governors can do some innovation at the state level. But there are constituencies that say the federal government shouldn't be involved in education, shouldn't be doing this, and consequently it should be done at the state level. **(Congressman Howard "Buck" McKeon, personal communication, February 27, 2008, on why the federal government can only play a minor role in innovation at the federal level)**

Educators often react negatively to business leaders telling them what to improve in schools and how it needs to be done. As a counterpoint, I propose that there are business leaders who could learn from educators, who work in a very different environment. Very few CEOs work so closely with their stakeholders and are governed by a board of people living in their community. And few, if any, educators have received the type of "bailout" support that the federal government gave businesses like Bear Stearns, Citibank, Fannie Mae, Freddie Mac, and General Motors for the business equivalent of failing to make adequate yearly progress under NCLB. The bailout was swift, sure, and lacking accountability, and one wonders what that amount of "free" money might mean to education.

To be sure, a number of businesses have gone through bankruptcy due to unexpected conditions that might have been beyond their control. (Some of the well-known names that didn't make it include Linens and Things, Sharper Image, Circuit City, and Ann Taylor.) Those companies that survived either found innovative ideas about operating in a brutally competitive business environment or wrote dramatically different business plans that sharply reduced costs. The same can be said of some schools that were forced to reconstitute under NCLB regulations. But the substantial financial assistance they needed wasn't available to them in the same way that it was for many failing businesses.

At the end of the day, the concepts of innovation embraced by businesses that successfully turned things around can be helpful to educators, and I hope that this chapter stimulates discussions about how to organize and implement innovation teams in schools. Modeling successful innovative business practices is a practical starting point.

> America's capacity to compete with China and the other economies that are growing is to produce people who are smarter, brighter, and more advanced. We still have a long way to go. We do this in our colleges. Our high schools and elementary schools are not setting kids up. And it's almost a cultural change. You can pass a law, but the law is not going to mean a lot. You can push the issue, but somehow you must generate more interest in education, especially in the home. We have to create more interest in the field of education that makes an immediate difference in the quality of the entire country in the fields that are producing cutting-edge knowledge: the sciences and math. We have a society that turns out more sports information people than physicists and chemists. That's not going to make us more competitive. **(Senator Judd Gregg, personal communication, June 12, 2007)**

> It will require applying the science of education, and I do not mean science education. We need to encourage using science in the learning process by using knowledge, evidence, and data. Using them should engage educators in teaching through an inquiry method. Using the science of learning and teaching could ultimately lead to innovation in education. **(Congressman Rush Holt, personal communication, May 8, 2008)**

There are a number of business writers and business leaders that offer insight into innovation that could inform initiatives in the field of education. IDEO is a company that focuses on design thinking and helps companies be more innovative. Some of the products and services that it helped develop include TiVo's digital recorder, the Swiffer CarpetFlick, and Bank of America's Keep the Change program. IDEO's work also includes designing for more complicated systemic challenges such as transforming the Kaiser Permanente healthcare system to be more patient centered, working with the Centers for Disease Control and Prevention to reduce childhood obesity, and developing a strategy for the Kellogg Foundation to improve early elementary education.

According to Tim Brown, IDEO's president and CEO, design thinking is an approach that uses the designer's sensibility and methods for problem solving to meet people's needs in a technologically feasible and commercially viable way. In other words, design thinking is human-centered innovation. Design thinking could be a powerful concept for the education reform innovation teams I have proposed. It is unfortunate that schools don't often have the discretionary funds to engage companies like IDEO in guiding them through an innovation activity. But it would still be possible to familiarize the innovation team with IDEO concepts and work to implement them. The work would be enhanced by professional development training and using an innovation coach to facilitate the team's activities.

IDEO approaches problems and innovation in three stages (see Figure 3.1). The first stage is inspiration, the background for which is a problem, opportunity, or both. Think about a school's problems or opportunities that are high priority and need to be a focus for the staff to resolve. According to IDEO's Sandy Speicher, the inspiration stage is very important because it is quite different from what most people typically do. It involves learning about and being inspired by people. IDEO approaches every challenge as an anthropologist would, which means going out and studying people in their homes and lives, and talking to them in order to reveal latent needs and motivations that help IDEO designers look at the challenge in a new way—one that is centered around people's needs, motivations, and behaviors.

Speicher expands on the details of the inspiration stage by saying that it involves far more than merely analyzing data, a process she suggests often leads to an answer that is "baked" in the way the data was compiled. IDEO's process uses a different type of data, seeking to learn about what people know, do, and care about in order to understand what the context for the challenge might be. Then, IDEO asks new questions and imagines new design solutions that often address a different need than what was assumed at the beginning.

Using the challenge of narrowing the achievement gap as an example, Speicher explains that IDEO might end up proposing solutions that are outside of school or engage other sources of the problem that are beyond what typical interventions focus on. The idea is to go beyond simply analyzing the data and approach the problem from an anthropological point of view with a "beginner's mind"—to be open to what you might discover beyond what you already know about the challenge at hand (Sandy Speicher, personal communication, March 30, 2009).

The second stage of IDEO's innovation process is ideation, during which the innovation team generates, develops, and tests ideas that could lead to a solution. The final stage is implementation, when the team actually develops and implements a plan. It should be noted that these stages are constantly being begun anew during the innovation

Figure 3.1   IDEO's Process of Innovation

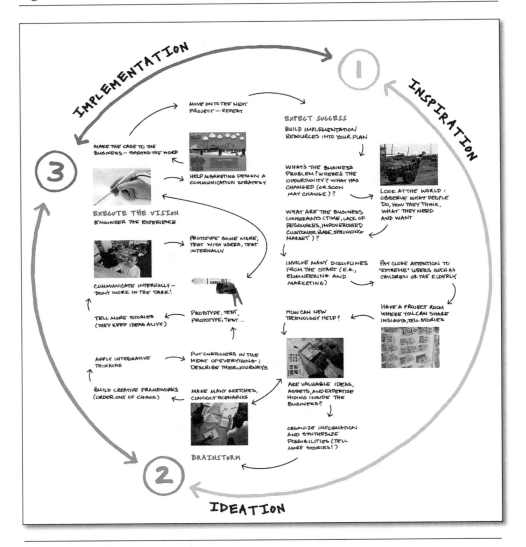

Courtesy of IDEO

process as new problems, ideas, and solutions are generated. It is an ongoing activity.

These three stages of innovation are not unlike a lot of work that is done in education. However, the process guided by IDEO often leads to breakthrough thinking that results in new processes and products. Unfortunately, innovation in education has not resulted in real breakthrough ideas that have led to large-scale success. Speicher speaks to why this sometimes happens:

Process is one thing you can go through without ever achieving the desired effect. You can go through an innovation process and never actually innovate. There are many reasons this may happen—often it's because it's quite difficult to break from the norms of the system. (personal communication, March 30, 2009)

Using the three stages of IDEO's innovation work—inspiration, ideation, and implementation—educators could look at a problem with a different perspective. Suppose closing the achievement gap is cited as the problem, and the IDEO process is used to begin seeking solutions.

Many questions need to be answered: Is there really a sincere desire in the school to close the achievement gap? Has the data that reflects the achievement gap been carefully analyzed by district leadership so that the innovation team can focus on a specific problem? Does the staff consider it a problem or an opportunity? And then there are the questions that the anthropology-minded researcher might ask: How do different students and families perceive of and value learning? What are the many activities that students and their families engage in throughout their day? How are both high-achieving and low-achieving students making decisions about how to spend their time and energy? Without a passionate commitment to change and a belief that the problem can be fixed, it is unlikely that an innovation team in a school district would be able to begin its work. After all, the first stage is inspiration.

And the next stage, ideation, requires generating ideas. But the very definition of innovation calls for those ideas to be new and "mold breaking." What solutions will the school's innovation team propose to use for narrowing the achievement gap? How are these solutions different from the methods that led to the gap in the first place? How carefully will the team use evidence-based ideas and new thinking to approach the old problem?

The last stage, implementation, calls for everyone working together to actually try the new ideas. The possibility that they might not work should not be considered a failure but rather an opportunity to learn from them. Then the team goes through the stages again. As Speicher says, fail early to succeed sooner.

In *The Ten Faces of Innovation,* Tom Kelley (2005), general manager at IDEO, discusses multiple roles that people take on in order to contribute to an innovation team. His list is very diverse, and the implication for education is to go beyond the traditional boundaries of the committee structures that group together people with similar responsibilities. For example, science curriculum committees are normally composed of science teachers. Kelley suggests that these groups need to consist of people with different backgrounds and organizes the 10 faces of innovation by personas, three of which are learning, organizing, and building. These include personality types such as experimenters, collaborators, directors, experience architects, and storytellers. Each of the personas brings a very different perspective to the work of the innovation team.

How would some of the personas be used in an education setting? Experimenters are the people who like to try different ideas and approaches. They are the ones who actually attempt to use the new ideas generated by the innovation team.

Collaborators are the people who bring everyone together to get things done. As Kelley (2005) describes them, "they coax people out of their silos to work together in multidisciplinary efforts" (p. 114).

Directors are the people who oversee the work and offer inspirational motivation to get things done. Successful directors generally possess five traits. They are able to let others get the attention, enjoy finding new projects, rise to tough challenges, have lofty goals, and possess a large toolbox of techniques, strategies, and resources.

Experience architects create conditions that stimulate thinking. They set the stage for positive encounters with the organization through multisensory experiences. A metaphor for educators to consider is the corner office with the view of a pond with trees and wildlife. How often do education meetings take place in rooms that do very little to stimulate creative thinking?

Finally, there are the storytellers. Storytelling is a powerful technique for leaders to use when trying to gain support from stakeholders. On innovation teams, stories provide a better context for explaining the goals for the work. Think of how different NCLB might have been perceived if it had been discussed in the same way President John Kennedy challenged America to put a man on the moon by the end of the decade. Rather than implementing a new law with the focus on the sanctions, think what might have happened had NCLB been introduced in such a way as to be embraced by educators as a challenge. I am not suggesting that sanctions were or are unnecessary. They are important, but a story about how so many of America's students have a limited chance to succeed in life because they didn't receive a good education would have been a better beginning for NCLB.

Kelley's (2005) *The 10 Faces of Innovation* would expand the thinking of education innovation teams and bring a wide diversity of viewpoints to the discussion. So innovation teams need to embrace all viewpoints and create a culture that brings new ideas to the solving of perplexing problems. It is important to point out that one face Kelley abhors is the devil's advocate, which he says is the biggest innovation killer in America.

Innovation is IDEO's business, and the concepts it uses are practical and applicable to education. Innovation teams can consist of a diverse group of personas, and these teams can cycle through the three innovation stages of design thinking to solve problems. Through effective leadership, the basic IDEO framework can be used to stimulate innovative thinking in any school or district.

Doblin is another innovation strategy company. It helps business leaders achieve their organization's full innovation potential by helping them assess their current innovation capabilities, improve innovation cycle times, and think beyond products to develop, select, and implement innovation concepts. And as with IDEO, there is reason to believe that applying some of the tools Doblin uses would benefit educators looking to innovate.

Doblin starts out with four categories: finance, process, offering, and delivery. Within these categories are 10 types of innovation: business model, networking, enabling process, core processes, product performance, product system, service, channel, brand, and customer experience (see Figure 3.2). This model calls for diagnosing the situation by taking several steps: developing a comprehensive view of the organizational need and the desire to innovate, declaring intent where leaders set direction (that is, affirming leader's vision), setting conditions under which it is likely that an innovation team will be given the opportunity to propose new and different ideas, coming up with and proposing initiatives, and fostering initiatives where they are implemented with a high degree of fidelity.

> Ideas, yes. Professional innovation companies specialize in developing great ideas, so I would certainly encourage the connection. I also see educators as well positioned to participate. They have the wonderful advantage of routine, meaningful contact with students, although their insights can be diluted by organizational realities. Professional firms can also help articulate their insights to get through those barriers. **(John Pipino, of Doblin, personal communication, March 26, 2009, on whether these companies could help educators generate bold, transformational ideas)**

In "Special Report: Innovation" (2008), *Inc.* magazine notes that "when people think about innovation, they tend to think about stuff. Bright, shiny, high-tech stuff that's patented, comes out of corporate research and development labs, and takes teams of engineers years of work and millions of dollars to develop" (p. 87). While the editors of the magazine really like those innovations, they are interested in the *how* and *what* of them as well. They note that innovation is

> less about gadgets and devices than it is about coming up with new ways to capture ideas, vet them, and bring them to market; about tapping the creativity of employees, customers, partners, even competitors . . . and constant incremental improvement in whatever it is a company does. (p. 87)

84

Figure 3.2

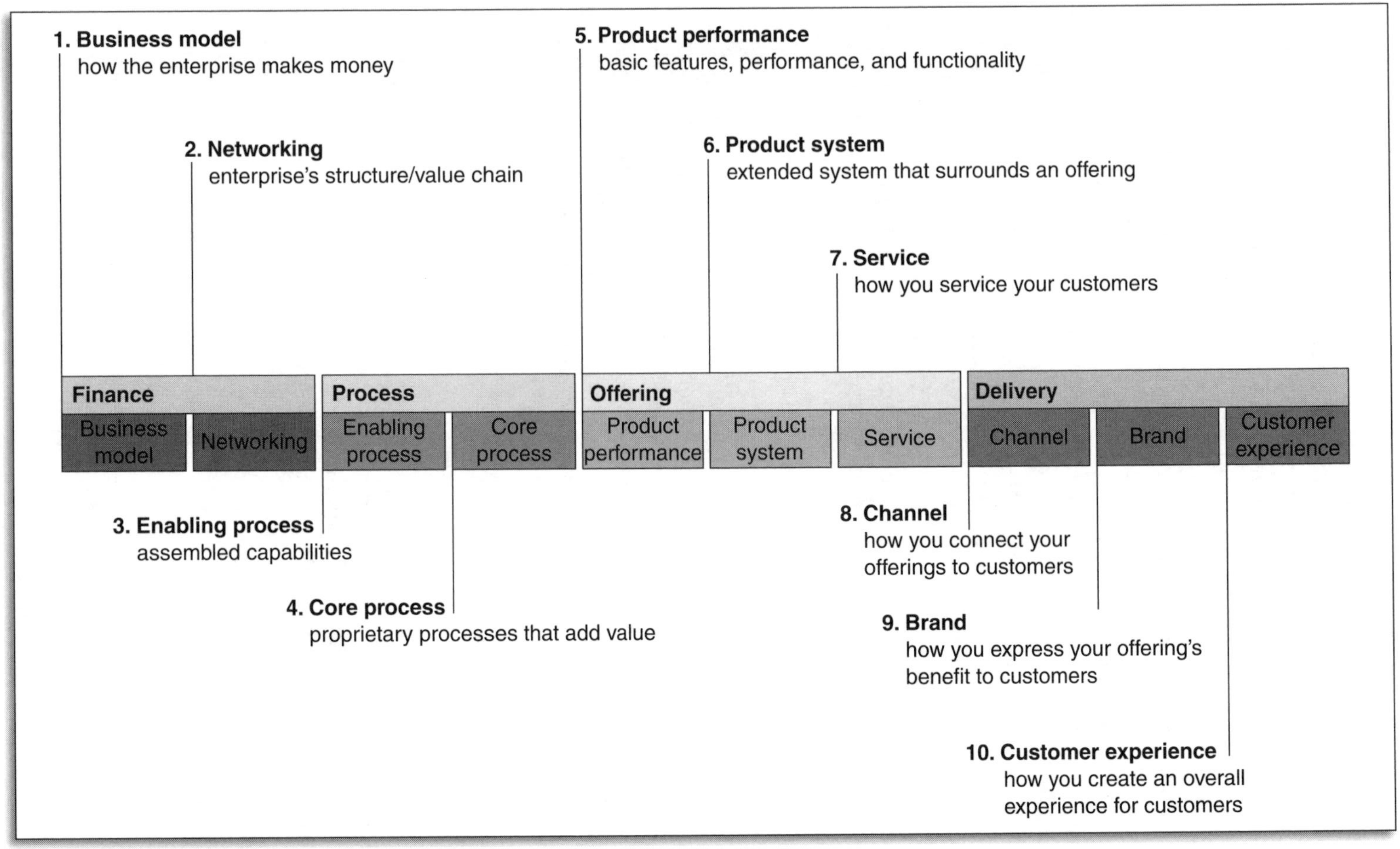

1. Business model
how the enterprise makes money

2. Networking
enterprise's structure/value chain

3. Enabling process
assembled capabilities

4. Core process
proprietary processes that add value

5. Product performance
basic features, performance, and functionality

6. Product system
extended system that surrounds an offering

7. Service
how you service your customers

8. Channel
how you connect your
offerings to customers

9. Brand
how you express your offering's
benefit to customers

10. Customer experience
how you create an overall
experience for customers

Finance	Process		Offering			Delivery		
Business model	Enabling process	Core process	Product performance	Product system	Service	Channel	Brand	Customer experience

Networking

Doblin Diagram reprinted with permission of Doblin Inc.

That type of thinking is particularly useful for education leaders looking to set a context for their innovation initiatives. Note the emphasis on capturing new ideas.

This book has discussed, among other things, the daunting challenge of complying with federal and state laws. It has also suggested that those compliance challenges are unlikely to disappear in the future. In fact, they are likely to present more complex and difficult challenges to educators with respect to accountability for ensuring students are learning the intended curriculum and demonstrating proficiency on assessments to validate their learning. *Inc.*'s approach to innovation is a good fit for education and supplements IDEO's process. The call for new ways to capture ideas and the notion that constant incremental improvement is conceptually a good plan supports the traditional method of how school teams work, but it also clearly encourages new thinking about how to solve ongoing problems.

Thomas Edison is considered to be one of the greatest inventors. His inventions were innovative and transformed the way people live and work. In *Innovate Like Edison,* Gelb and Caldicott (2007) discuss the five competencies of innovation:

- solution-centered mindset
- kaleidoscopic thinking
- full-spectrum engagement
- mastermind collaboration
- super-value creation

Each of these competencies aligns with goals. Applying the concept of the competencies and goals to education innovation teams provides a structure for stimulating new and different thinking. The solution-centered mindset goals, for example, are to align goals and passions, cultivate charismatic optimism, seek knowledge relentlessly, experiment persistently, and pursue rigorous objectivity. None of these is inconsistent with the work educators do on a daily basis. How can these goals be used in a school to stimulate innovation that would encourage different approaches to solving a problem?

Innovators have to be passionate about their work, and it is critically important for the staff to feel passionate about resolving the issues that confront them. If narrowing the achievement gap is the goal, a willingness to experiment persistently in order to achieve that goal it is essential. The willingness to pursue rigorous objectivity should not be overlooked. There is often too much ideology involved in education work, and the willingness to put that ideology aside can lead to more open thinking for innovative solutions. Specifically, I am referring to the constant battle between the whole language and phonics advocates in the realm of literacy and between the different mathematics groups debating computational skills and problem solving. Those types of battles, and the team member who plays devil's advocate, will bring real innovative thinking to an abrupt halt.

Kaleidoscopic thinking is a concept that Gelb and Caldicott (2007) associate with Edison's approach to idea generation. They say kaleidoscopic thinkers maintain a notebook, practice ideaphoria, discern patterns, express ideas visually, and explore roads not taken. There is nothing remarkably new or unusually challenging here for an education innovation team. Of critical importance, though, is that for innovative ideas to develop, it is important to explore roads not taken. For years, many of the problems confronting education have not been corrected. Generally, there is a belief that experimentation and radically new ideas are not good strategies. While it is true that failing to make progress can have serious consequences for a school, the fact is that year after year of getting the same results is evidence that something new and different needs to be tried. Kaleidoscopic thinking, or whatever else one may want to call it, is essential to innovation work.

Intensity and relaxation, seriousness and playfulness, sharing and protecting, complexity and simplicity, and solitude and team are the elements of full-spectrum engagement. These pairings are obviously opposites and suggest that to be successful you have to be fully engaged and allow for each element to be embraced by the members of the innovation team. Gelb and Caldicott (2007) describe Edison fully engaging in his work "with the least amount of friction and with the whole momentum of his mind" (p. 115). It is important for leaders to create conditions that stimulate innovative thinking. An innovation team that uses all of these paired elements and balances them to appropriately achieve its goals will have a greater chance of successfully coming up with new and innovative ideas.

Bringing a diverse group of people together with different intelligences who share the same passions and goals is mastermind collaboration. This involves recruiting for chemistry and results, designing multidisciplinary collaboration teams, inspiring an environment of open exchange, rewarding collaboration, and becoming a master networker. Conceptually, this is similar to IDEO's inspiration stage and use of an anthropological approach.

The last Edison competency that Gelb and Caldicott (2007) discuss is super-value creation. Although it has more of a business overtone to it, thinking of it in an education context is still possible. The activities involved include linking market trends with core strengths, tuning in to target audiences, applying the right business model, understanding scale-up effects, and creating an unforgettable market-moving brand. A school innovation team would need to create some hybrid activities to align with this competency. Taking the example of closing the achievement gap, the starting point for the team would be determining how to scale up effort throughout the school or district. If narrowing the achievement gap is a high priority, then the team would begin considering how to implement its work systemically. The team would need to identify the core strengths of what is currently being done successfully and how those strengths could be coupled with new ideas that lead to higher achievement for students who don't meet the district's expectations. The innovation team might ask questions such as these: Who are those target audiences? What model can be applied throughout the system that would bring a consistency of effort? Finally, the team would carefully analyze the trends of districts that have been successful, and that information would inform its work.

It is like an epiphany when one begins to analyze the Edison innovation competencies and how similar they are to what IDEO and *Inc.* magazine say about innovation. A clearer picture of the innovation process for an education innovation team is beginning to emerge. That picture includes analyzing evidence about the problem, encouraging diverse viewpoints, recruiting members with different backgrounds, providing opportunities for open and shared communication, taking risks, and working with a knowledge and evidence base that will make the innovation discussions productive and useful. On the other hand, discussing fads and ideologies would be a lot like encouraging the devil's advocate conversation.

Innovation is often thought of as a game changer—much like pulling a suitcase on wheels as opposed to carrying it. One of the more dramatic game changers has been the Internet. Think about how it has changed the way you do many daily tasks. You purchase commodities using a computer, and they are delivered directly to your home. You can compare prices online to ensure you get the best deal. Just those two tasks alone have had a significant impact on bricks-and-mortar businesses, which have had to reduce prices in order to compete.

Another innovative change is how people access the news. Newspapers and magazines are undergoing the most significant innovation transformation since the printing press was invented. Many people now access their newspaper online, maybe via Amazon's Kindle electronic reader or their cell phones. The concept of the newspaper being delivered to your door is rapidly disappearing. To survive and retain their core business, these established print media industries have had to innovate and will have to continue doing so.

Lafley and Charan (2008) define the game changer as having seven basic ideas. For education, I have selected four of these that could be used as the foundation of thinking for an innovation team:

- a visionary strategist who alters the game his business plays or conceives of an entirely new game
- a leader who understands that the consumer or customer, not the CEO, is boss
- an integrator who sees innovation as an integrated end to end process, not a series of discrete steps
- a hardheaded humanist who sees innovation as a social process and understands that human interaction—how people talk and work together—is the key to innovation, not just technology (p. vii)

Lafley and Charan (2008) describe an innovation process that could be used quite effectively in education, which is consistent with the ideas discussed earlier in this chapter. They call it the *theatre of innovation*. The theatre is an old brewery called Clay Street. It is a think tank playground and has desks, whiteboards, computers, and conference areas with crayons, toys, other items. It is run by a person whose background includes theatrical director, designer, and engineer. Clay Street is actually what I think is necessary for creating the conditions to stimulate education innovation. It is also the antithesis to what I mentioned earlier about using classrooms for education innovation teams to do their work. Educators need to be provided with an environment that will stimulate innovation, an area that isn't where they do their work every day.

The process begins with a Procter & Gamble executive identifying a problem related to growth that links to the company's business strategy. Then 8–12 people are assembled into a team and released from their usual work duties for several weeks. That alone is different from the traditional approach to solving problems in education, where the teams often meet after school or for a day when they are released from their work duties. And even when they are released from their duties for a day, they still have to prepare lesson plans and deal with problems that may have arisen during the day with their substitute teacher.

The P&G team consists of people with diverse backgrounds and some outsiders who are often more likely to make comments that employees might not make. Lafley and Charan (2008) note that if it is a marketing project, there will be team members from finance, human resources, and other departments. The team members will vary by age and gender, and they will be from different cities and countries. Again, the diversity is consistent with everything that was suggested earlier in the chapter about how important it is to get different perspectives for innovation.

The team's first task is to build their collective knowledge. They also work on fostering a trust relationship. Over time, they begin focusing on the business problem they are trying to solve with innovative ideas and invite speakers to help them expand their thinking. After working in Clay Street, participants acknowledge that they have a better ability to connect unrelated ideas and design creative experiments to make breakthroughs, which they could not have done alone.

Think of how this type of opportunity might apply to an education innovation team trying to close the achievement gap. Suppose a school organizes a team that is solely working on closing the achievement gap in mathematics. But the team has not only mathematics teachers but also parents of students from different ethnic backgrounds as well as physical education, art, and music teachers. How could the innovation coach create instructional strategy discussions that elicit new ideas from those who don't teach mathematics but that still address the problems of the students who have not reached acceptable achievement levels? What ideas might the parents suggest that have not been explored? Might a physical education, art, or music teacher introduce a new topic using learning strategies that are different from what the mathematics teachers have been using?

Lafley and Charan (2008) cite IDEO's seven rules for brainstorming, a discussion process that is essential to producing innovation thinking:

- Defer judgment.
- Encourage wild ideas.
- Build on the ideas of others.
- Stay focused on the topic.
- [Have] one conversation at a time.
- Be visual.
- Go for quantity. (p. 246)

Lafley and Charan (2008) add to these their 10 rules for effective brainstorming:

1. *Get a facilitator.* I recommend that the facilitator be the school district's innovation coach. There should be an understanding that the coach has been prepared to lead and facilitate the innovating thinking process.

2. *Be prepared.* For a school innovation team to accomplish a lot of work in a brief period of time, it is important for team members to come to meetings prepared to work and not attempt to read the background material during meetings.

3. *Relax.* This includes discouraging negative comments. This rule goes back to IDEO's rejection of a devil's advocate discussion and how important it is to create the proper environment for innovation thinking and discussion.

4. *Leaders should follow.* The goal of a brainstorming session is to encourage open discussion. It is a good practice for formal organizational leaders to be less visible during brainstorming so that everyone senses a good opportunity to participate in discussions. When leaders attend brainstorming discussions, it can have a chilling effect on participants' willingness to engage in open discussion.

5. *Get everyone to contribute.* A good facilitator should be able to engage all members of the group.

6. *Keep track of ideas.* All ideas should be considered essential to innovation thinking. Whether they are maintained on chart paper, interactive whiteboards, or computers, it is critically important for the group to discuss and consider all of them.

7. *Think ahead.* This rule stipulates that brainstorming is a beginning, not an end. Lafley and Charan (2008) note that it is important to generate

ideas, connect them, and then repeat the process. Innovation doesn't start and stop. It is about building a school culture in which new ideas for solving serious problems are constantly being sought.

8. *Use props.* IDEO calls this *prototyping.* It is when the team uses products, processes, or artifacts to demonstrate how their ideas could be implemented. Prototyping means using the innovation being considered and evaluating how it works.

9. *Go beyond the lines.* In education, we often refer to out-of-the-box thinking. Whatever it is called, innovation work must be really different. The goal is to try bold, new ideas. Remember what Sandy Speicher from IDEO said about failing early to succeed sooner.

10. *Follow the rules.* Not following a basic plan is unlikely to lead to innovation and successful results.

These rules that Lafley and Charan (2008) propose are sensible and outline a brainstorming framework for innovation thinking. With these and IDEO's rules, an education innovation team has what it needs to get started on solving a problem using a different method than the traditional inside-the-box solutions that are often proposed and that have limited success. It is important to emphasize that I have taken just a small excerpt from the theatre of innovation. A more comprehensive and detailed overview can be found in Lafley and Charan's *The Game-Changer.*

One of the world's leading innovation companies is Toyota. In *The Elegant Solution,* Matthew May (2007), senior advisor to the University of Toyota, discusses the company as one that is "always seeking to find and fit the rhythm of the change happening around it" (p. ix). Toyota is a company that believes good enough is never enough. It seeks to improve employee productivity, engagement, continuous improvement, and constant creativity. Think about how powerful those four concepts could be for a school innovation team trying to solve a challenging problem in a culture that cultivates that type of thinking.

As I noted earlier, innovation can be complex or simple. It can be about products, processes, or programs. Toyota believes business innovation is about satisfaction and value, and the company defines innovation as trying to figure out "a way to do something better than it's ever been done before" (May, 2007, p. 49). Applying this definition to a school innovation team's mission provides the basis for why the team is meeting in the first place. Education innovation should be about getting better. Toyota's approach to innovation involves three principles:

- the art of ingenuity
- the pursuit of perfection
- the rhythm of fit

Practicing the art of ingenuity is about creative thinking and is accomplished through brainstorming sessions. It is analogous to the ideation step at IDEO. It is the opportunity for the school innovation team to put new and creative ideas on the table in order to solve those vexing problems that have prevented the school from achieving its anticipated success.

Pursuing perfection is the ultimate goal of innovation. How can educators continue to build on their body of knowledge through innovative thinking to achieve that goal? Since NCLB was passed with the goal that 100% of students would achieve proficiency by 2014, the debate has been about why this is nearly impossible to do. An appropriate goal would be to align accountability with the pursuit of perfection and recognize that not all students will achieve it. Acknowledging this fact is really no different than recognizing that not all patients undergoing surgery by the world's best heart surgeon are going to survive or that every National Football League team can win the Super Bowl. While it may be politically unacceptable to say it, on balance the pursuit of perfection using accountability measures is what will stimulate innovative thinking.

May (2007) describes the rhythm of fit as the right thing at the right time in the right form for the right people. Schools cannot continue to do things the way they have been done in the past. That doesn't mean they should discard practices, products, or programs with clear, unarguable evidence that they work, but they do need to acknowledge that the world has moved from analog to digital and the importance of that transition. Just as Congressman Miller said, analog schools have to become digital and their staffs have to leave their comfort zone.

It is striking to observe the similarity of the steps in the innovation processes used by different businesses. The fact that the steps are not radically different means that educators can learn from what businesses have done to successfully build innovation into their operational culture and then modify it to meet their contextual situations.

May (2007) outlines several steps in the innovation process embraced at Toyota:

1. *Let learning lead.* The 21st century calls for a knowledge-based workforce. It is simply not logical to assume that an education innovation team is going to produce new and different ideas without a solid knowledge base about its work. One of the leading proponents for building a knowledge culture in education is Jim Kohlmoos, president of Knowledge Alliance, a nonprofit, nonpartisan strategic alliance that addresses the need to apply rigorous research to persistent education challenges facing our country's schools. (In the interest of full disclosure, my employer, Learning Point Associates, is a member of Knowledge Alliance, and I serve as a board and executive committee member of the organization.)

> Knowledge generated from a robust research and development infrastructure has been the lifeblood of innovation and increased productivity in many sectors such as agriculture, energy, medicine, and defense. American education's hopes for significant improvement and systemic change depend upon how new research-based knowledge is created and used in solving real problems facing our schools. Knowledge utilization should be an essential part of any reform strategy that seeks to scale up and sustain improvement over time. **(Jim Kohlmoos, personal communication, September 22, 2008, on why knowledge utilization is so important to education)**

2. *Learn to see.* Similar to IDEO's concept of using an anthropological approach, the Toyota practice suggests that it is important to get out more and live in the world you are trying to improve. This could have a profound impact on education because most planning for instructional services in schools is not done with a clear understanding of the diverse interests of students. As student populations become more diverse, there is a need to better understand who is receiving the education and what would work best for them.

3. *Design for today.* An innovation team needs to focus on present needs and be certain that they are not manufacturing them. The team needs to be certain that the problem they are working on will resolve a current issue, not a plan for the future. For educators, this means using data and evidence to identify the most serious problems and then determine what the innovation team will try to improve.

4. *Think in pictures.* I have mentioned mindsets as important for innovation work. May (2007) refers to the work of Edward Tufte, who has done some excellent work on visually displaying quantitative information. May emphasizes the importance of mental images. A good example would be how presenters use PowerPoint presentations. Do you remember presentations that gave you interesting graphical depictions of what was being said and some that were only narrative?

5. *Capture the intangible.* May (2007) notes that the most compelling solutions are often perceptual and emotional. Getting diverse thinking from the innovation team will be useful in acquiring that type of thinking. What would you attempt if you knew you couldn't fail? May says that this is a trick question because you can't fail in the attempt, only the outcome.

6. *Leverage the limits.* The notion here is that there is an addiction to abundant resources, and that is not necessarily the best way to innovate. Innovation work should not be about spending large sums of money. In fact, not having such resources might lead to better solutions.

7. *Master the tension.* The team needs to work through creative tension. "Breakthrough thinking comes from breaking through the mental barrier erected by the obvious solutions" (May, 2007, p 145).

8. *Run the numbers.* The team must avoid relying on insight and instinct, and instead focus on facts. Using data can help avoid bias and instinct. The team should be certain to use relevant data and really focus on the problem they are trying to solve.

9. *Make kaizen mandatory.* While perfection is often not the goal in education work, *kaizen* (Japanese for endless improvement and innovation) calls for creating a standard, following it, and finding a better way. "Trying to improve and innovate without a standard as reference is like a journey with no starting point" (May, 2007, p 167).

10. *Keep it lean.* The team should not make the work complex. Simple solutions like a suitcase with wheels can be transformational. It is likely that there are many innovative ideas waiting to be cultivated in the right conditions in many schools. Educators should not discount the value of their institutional knowledge. One problem might be that they have not had the opportunity to work in a real innovation environment to prototype their ideas and apply them to an authentic setting.

It should be noted that the education examples I highlight later in the chapter are only examples of innovation and likely did not result from intentional innovation design work. What is most important to remember is that innovation means different things to different people. Education innovators are trying to solve problems that are often contextual to their particular situation. Consequently, what might pass as an innovation in one school or district might not be considered innovative in another school or district.

Yet many educators who are devising innovative and effective solutions to problems in their specific settings could help colleagues in other contexts. One problem with the decentralized system of education in the United States is that not many other educators learn about those successful innovations, which means they can't replicate them. Getting this information disseminated on a much larger scale is essential to helping other educators struggling with similar problems. Just figuring out how to move innovative ideas throughout the education profession would be an incredibly useful innovation.

It is interesting to note that a "majority of voters say that developing students' imagination and creativity are important to innovation and success in a knowledge-based economy" (Sawchuk, 2008, p. 3). This finding supports the need for schools to begin focusing on new ways of educating students that are aligned to trends that are emerging in the 21st-century global environment. Some of those trends include social networking using digital communication, working collaboratively in teams, solving problems through creative thinking, and leading in a way that connects with followers. Only through innovation will bold, new ideas emerge.

Time magazine published a cover story on preparing schools and students for the 21st century (Wallis, 2006). The article supports the importance of competencies in traditional academic disciplines, but also calls for students to be competent in knowing about the world, thinking outside the box, becoming smarter about new sources of information, and developing good people skills.

In an op ed that appeared in the *Los Angeles Times,* Cory Booker, John Doerr, and Ted Mitchell (2008) said, "We need a new, results-driven mindset at the Department of Education that will drive pure educational innovation and 'scale up' proven experiments and novel ideas that work. The federal government stands in a unique position to meet these needs" (para. 6). (Booker is the mayor of Newark, New Jersey; Doerr is a partner in a venture capital firm; and Mitchell is chief executive of New Schools Venture Fund and president of the California Board of Education.) These three individuals have influence, and their call for innovation in education, supported by the federal government and coupled with a Broad Foundation initiative, is the type of activity that could make a difference in helping educators achieve better results in schools and districts.

In an op ed for the *Philadelphia Inquirer,* I point out that "stimulating the education sector to innovate will not be easy, but nothing will contribute more to our nation's vitality" (Kimmelman, 2007). I also suggest a few simple steps:

- Invest more in research and development.
- Invite more collaboration among businesses, academia, research organizations, and education leaders to stimulate new approaches to vexing challenges.
- Offer merit-based grants to states that develop winning approaches to teacher preparation, instructional methods, and public/private partnerships to disseminate their know-how across the profession.

Most of the calls for innovation in education suggest engaging in more research and development, finding new ideas to solve the challenging issue of the achievement gap, improving teacher quality, developing better data systems, and collaborating with partners who have specialized interests both in and out of education and better processes for getting their work distributed more widely in the field. But first there needs to be a conceptual framework for educators to use to even begin the innovation process.

AN EDUCATION INNOVATION PROCESS FRAMEWORK

Some of the great innovations used today are really simple. Wheeled suitcases was an incredibly simple idea that makes getting around much easier for travelers and even those hauling heavy business cases during their daily routines. The paper clip was also a practical innovation and is still commonly used by people who want to organize and hold their papers together. These ideas are truly metaphors for what might emerge from education innovation teams.

In this section, I describe a framework for organizing a district or school innovation team that can easily be modified to fit a variety of contexts (see Figure 3.3). It is not intended as something that must be rigidly followed, but instead it should be used to implement a process that will lead to innovative

Figure 3.3   The Process of Innovation

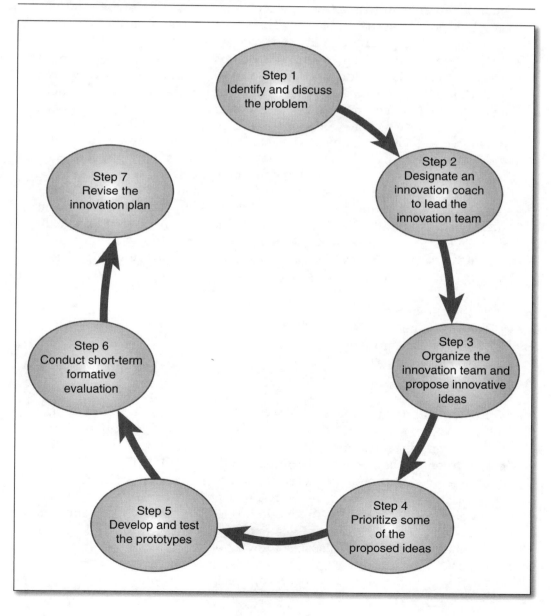

ideas for solving critical problems in districts and schools. What is most important is that the team focuses on solving a problem and is willing to consider bold ideas that seem unachievable. As Sandy Speicher from IDEO says, you can learn from failure. What you learn becomes the foundation for using knowledge to improve what you tried. It also means that it might be better to continue with the original idea rather than doing what happens so often in education—discarding it for another new idea and starting over again. You don't build on knowledge by constantly starting over.

It is important to emphasize that the innovation team is different from the traditional curriculum committee or other similar committees in schools. The innovation team works from the problem to build prototype solutions using bold ideas and new thinking. The team focuses on developing new products, practices, and programs and/or new ways of using them.

The term *team* is often overused and identifies working groups as teams that actually do not function as a team. According to Katzenbach and Smith (2006), a team is "a small number of people with complementary skills who are committed to a common purpose, performance goals, and approach for which they hold themselves mutually accountable" (p. 45). The innovation team must be passionate about its work and committed to working collaboratively to achieve what many believe is not possible. And the team must hold itself accountable for its work.

As a caution, it helps to be reminded about what Lencioni (2002) identifies as the five dysfunctions of a team. Adding knowledge of this to what Katzenbach and Smith (2006) say is essential for a high-performance team will provide the innovation team leader with a much greater chance of success when undertaking the responsibility for team leadership. These are Lencioni's five dysfunctions of a team:

- absence of trust
- fear of conflict
- lack of commitment
- avoidance of accountability
- inattention to results (p. 188)

Implementing an innovation process will be different in every district and school. Some will have the resources to hire consultants to offer professional training in leadership and innovation. Those fortunate enough to be able to enlist the services of companies like IDEO or Doblin have an advantage because they will receive expert technical support. Other districts and schools may not have the resources to hire consultants and may simply use this book and the innovation process framework to form their own learning community to implement an innovation team. While it is unfortunate that not all districts and schools have the discretionary resources to hire consultants, remember this: you can still get to the same destination whether you fly first class or coach. I am confident that district and school innovation teams, when properly facilitated, can devise innovative ideas that will lead to improvements.

Creating an innovative culture requires leadership from the superintendent and her team to ensure that the staff assigned to lead innovation teams has adequate preparation and resources, authority to make decisions, and support to achieve their goals. It doesn't have to be a costly process. Funds currently used to finance curricular committees or other instructional activities can be diverted for this purpose. If innovation work is considered a priority, then it means scrutinizing the current budget to find the available funding.

Step 1: Identify and Discuss the Problem

The first step in the innovation process is for school or district leaders to identify and discuss the problem. There must be a sense that a problem actually exists. Once the problem is identified, the leaders should discuss it using data and/or emerging programs, products, or practices as the starting point to give the innovation team some direction. While this is the first step for the innovation process, it does not actually involve the innovation team. At this point, the district or school leaders should be analyzing the priority issues and preparing the background material for the innovation team to use. Separating the identification of the problem and the solution will bring different perspectives that are important for stimulating innovative thinking.

The problem should be identified using credible and relevant data and/or becoming aware of a new product, program, or practice that has been subjected to an acceptable research process to affirm that it can work effectively in a demographic setting similar to that of the district's or school's. Data is compelling evidence and can be used to identify and help educators focus on a problem. If a school discovers it has poor student attendance and continues to analyze the data to get at the core problem, it can begin to think about creative ways to solve it. If mathematics achievement is higher in one grade level than in another, data can help isolate possible problems. If overall student achievement is not as good as expected, data can help innovation teams think about creative solutions by reframing the key issues. And if new products, programs, or practices offer promise, they should be integrated into the discussion.

For example, one new idea in education that is innovative in its use of personnel data is the focus on human capital resource management. The idea is that merging human resource offices with curriculum and instruction departments provides a more integrated and comprehensive portal of staff information for reviewing student achievement issues. Districts typically do not connect all the human resource management functions in a way that provides stewardship for the critical human talent that drives student performance. What if disappointing student achievement is the result of inadequate professional development for teachers working with a new instructional program, and it was overlooked because different departments handled curriculum program recommendations and professional development approvals? Like putting wheels on a suitcase, two products, or in this instance departments, are merged, at the very least creating a communication network between them. This action could prevent a serious problem regarding student achievement. The combined data from personnel and curriculum/instruction uses not only information about teachers and student achievement but also the financial resources supporting their work. It simply means looking at the problem systemically with a different mindset about how the administration operates.

Using data to identify a problem necessitates looking at the data with a different mindset. Despite the fact that this step in the process isn't necessarily carried out with the innovation team, it is an essential beginning to using innovation to solve a problem. Nancy Love (2009) offers an interesting and contemporary collaborative process in *Using Data to Improve Learning for All*. She talks about using data "to turn the challenges of accountability into our greatest opportunity" (p. ix), a notion that clearly supports the concept of using innovation teams to work on the most critical problems after the leaders have identified them. Love discusses three findings about collaborative inquiry. The first is that it has the power to solve the biggest problem confronting schools in the era of increased accountability and improving teaching and learning.

The second requires a wholesale cultural change in schools, which is crucial to innovative thinking. The notion that nothing is impossible and a willingness to explore bold and different ideas requires that an innovation team have members with the mindset of wanting to climb Mt. Everest. Simply stated, you must have lofty goals.

The third finding is that collaborative inquiry is based on more than data. As noted earlier in this chapter, when Sandy Speicher discussed the inspiration stage at IDEO, using data is one method of identifying a problem, but new products, programs, and practices are constantly emerging. They, too, represent an important part of the solution identification process. In a world that is changing constantly, in which the quest to stay competitive plays out on a daily basis, scanning for what is new and promising cannot be considered an annual activity but instead must also take place daily. The Internet brings incredible information to users every minute of the day, and while monitoring for new information on a daily basis may be too cumbersome a task for someone who doesn't have the time, it is important to be keenly aware of how quickly new information becomes available.

Step 2: Designate an Innovation Coach to Lead the Innovation Team

As noted earlier, the team needs to be diverse and it must be willing to offer bold, new ideas from different perspectives, recognize that nothing is impossible, and take some risks. The team also should be willing to move away from any resemblance to the traditional culture of education teams working on improvement initiatives. Innovation is clearly about change. Innovative ideas are not guaranteed to be successful, but they do present new perspectives to solving problems and can ultimately lead to a successful solution.

Steven Prokesch (2009) discusses why General Electric is so successful in creating teams that bring about change:

- Team training accelerated the pace of training by giving managers an opportunity to reach consensus on the barriers to change and how best to work on them.
- Participants considered the hard barriers to change, essentially organizational, and the soft barriers, essentially how the members of the team individually and collectively behaved.
- [The team] simultaneously manag[ed] the present while creating the future.
- The team created a common vocabulary of change that became part of daily communication systemically.
- The program was not an academic exercise, and the team would present a first draft of an action plan for the change and then feel obligated to deliver on it. (Prokesch, 2009, pp. 1–2)

Once the district or school leaders have identified the problem, they can hand it off to an innovation coach. I recommend that teachers be designated as innovation coaches to lead the innovation team. Properly training teachers to be team leaders in leadership and innovation concepts will result in teams that function more effectively. These positions do not have to be full-time. Obviously, it would not be a good use of resources to train someone for a one-time activity, but training a cadre of teachers who can lead an innovation team from time to time doesn't place the burden on one person and contributes to a better organizational culture by having a number of people thinking about innovation and leadership. Further, it supports the trend of giving teachers leadership opportunities and the training to support them.

Think about some of the products you use daily; it is likely that they were developed over time and have been consistently improved through small changes. Tackling a broad education problem, such as teaching English to non-English-speaking students, could take years, but using innovative thinking, consistently improving innovation, and sustaining the effort is much better than starting over year after year with a new product, program, or practice.

The team should be led by a coach who has been trained in leadership and innovation concepts. It isn't essential for the training to come from a higher education degree-granting program, but the team leader must be adequately prepared to work with a diverse team in processing bold ideas and designing prototypes to test them in authentic situations. It would be beneficial for smaller districts to collaborate on this training and use well-respected consulting services that do a good job of offering the type of training that results in effective innovation work. Larger school districts will likely be able to do this independently. With the emphasis on innovation, it is also likely that federal funding will be increased to support it.

The overview on leadership in Chapter 2 contains the basic concepts of education leadership that can be the core of the training program. The beginning of this chapter is fundamentally an overview of the concepts of innovation. This basic understanding of leadership and innovation, and possibly some additional work with consultants who update the information and provide scenario training, should be sufficient for a team leader to engage in a meaningful innovation team activity.

Step 3: Organize the Innovation Team and Propose Innovative Ideas

The innovation coach now organizes the team. Getting a diverse group of people together is critically important to generating bold, new ideas. Just as IDEO employs people with very different backgrounds, the district or school innovation team should be composed of people from different teaching disciplines. It would also be beneficial to consider asking noneducators to participate on the team in order to get ideas that are not normally considered in an education setting. Innovation means breaking away from the traditional methods of doing things and considering new ways of attacking a problem. While the team will be using the data that identified the problem, the bold, new ideas should highlight different products, practices, and programs. The team should consist of members who will be able to contribute that type of thinking. They need to be respectful of everyone's ideas and not inject "killer" statements. Remember the IDEO rejection of a devil's advocate. All ideas need to be considered at the outset.

For example, imagine that the team is working on the problem of lower-than-acceptable student scores in eighth-grade mathematics. The traditional process would be to assign a group of mathematics teachers to develop an improvement plan. The difference between the traditional team and the innovation team, however, is one of composition. The innovation team should include, in addition to the mathematics teachers, possibly an art teacher, a music teacher, a physical education teacher, and others who don't view the problem through the lens of a mathematics educator. The perspectives of these teachers might provide epiphanies. It may also be helpful to include parents, students, business representatives, local policymakers, and others who will offer a very different perspective.

The team needs to believe that it can solve any problem brought before it. Achieving what might be perceived as impossible should not present an obstacle. The mindset for the team should be the same as NASA's Apollo 13 team, which found a solution to a very serious problem and successfully brought Captain James Lovell and his crew back to earth when it appeared there was no possibility of fixing their spacecraft. When it seemed like there was no hope, the team leader assigned to find a solution made it very clear that "failure is not an option." That now-famous phrase is an excellent metaphor for education innovation team activities. To achieve the type of success necessary to ensure that all students perform at intended achievement levels, it is incredibly important to have a mindset that it is possible.

Step 4: Prioritize Some of the Proposed Ideas

It is now time for the coach to confront the most difficult challenge of the team process. The team must take all of the proposed ideas and begin to winnow them down to a workable number, probably no more than two or three. The coach must be able to keep the team functioning effectively while eliminating some of the ideas offered by its members. In this step especially, the team leader must understand Bruce Tuckman's (1965) team development model, whereby teams go through a series of stages: forming, storming, norming, performing, and adjourning.

While winnowing down the ideas, the team may go through the storming stage because some ideas are discarded and factions of the team may vie for power. The storming stage is when the team confronts the reality of how difficult it is to make decisions. It is when the presence of a skilled and trained leader is essential in order to help the team focus on its primary innovation goal and negotiate compromises to keep the team functioning effectively.

The storming stage is why I emphatically highlight the need to offer training to teacher leaders in both leadership and innovation. They must be properly prepared for this assignment and able to guide the team through not only this stage, but the other stages as well.

Once the team has agreed on the limited number of innovation ideas that it will work with, it needs to specifically define the desired outcomes for each one. The outcomes must be very clear so that the innovation can be accurately evaluated. Rather than discarding an idea, innovation necessitates a firm commitment to continuously working to improve what is being done. Naturally, I am not suggesting that an innovation that clearly hasn't worked continue to be used, but innovation necessitates some trial and error to get it right.

Reducing the number of ideas is essential because during the next step of the innovation framework, the team is going to develop the prototypes that will be tested. Managing more than two or three prototypes would be too difficult.

Finally, new ideas and practices often result in controversy in schools. While avoiding controversy is sometimes impossible, during this step it is important to communicate to all stakeholders what is being done and why, with the specific intent of gaining support for the work. Experimentation in schools is unnerving for parents and some staff, so building a supportive coalition should be considered an important priority.

Step 5: Develop and Test the Prototypes

The innovation team's decision regarding what ideas to use will become the basis for the prototypes, which will be the structure for the innovation. It is the complete process for how the innovation will be implemented. Of critical importance is to be sure to have some measurable goals for evaluating the prototype. The team must be specific regarding what it hopes to accomplish.

Let's consider that an innovation team is working on the problem of students at one grade level not achieving the intended proficiency. The team develops two possible innovative scenarios that might result in higher achievement. They reach this conclusion after reviewing the data and analyzing what is currently being done. Then they discuss some ideas that would radically change the way the target population of students is taught. They agree that a bold, new plan should be used because the data indicate that this grade level of students has not achieved proficiency over a three-year period. They decide on two ideas.

The team them begins the task of constructing a comprehensive implementation plan. This includes a complete review of the scenario from when the student enters the classroom until the class ends. It also incorporates ideas about supportive activities in the home and other classes the students attend. Overall, teachers are going to be offered support for different instructional strategies, a laboratory environment in which to work with colleagues on instructional strategies, new resource materials, and integrating technology applications. The prototype will be used for a period of time, evaluated, and compared to the other innovation idea being tested.

Prototypes should be carefully planned. They should be defined and clarified in a highly detailed manner. Nothing should be left to assuming what should be done. By implementing the innovation with fidelity, the innovation team will be able to evaluate the results more accurately and make decisions based on credible evidence.

Step 6: Conduct Short-Term Formative Evaluation

Now the innovation team collaborates with others in the district to help evaluate the results of using the prototype. The evaluation is short term, most likely one school year, but can be compared to previous results from the program currently being used and the other prototype being evaluated. Each prototype evaluation must include specific objectives that were intended outcomes. The primary purpose of innovating is to try bold, new ideas that produce improved results over time. The short-term formative evaluation enables the team to monitor results of the changes on a continuous basis and modify implementation procedures that are not working as intended.

Step 7: Revise the Innovation Plan

What often happens in schools when significant changes are implemented and the results are not what were hoped for is that the product, program, or practice is discarded. Innovation, as noted earlier, requires time and continuous analysis of the implementation so that appropriate modifications can be made as the team learns more about how it is working. The innovation process was initiated to solve a significant problem, and it should be understood that an innovative process may take some time to achieve the anticipated results. The team should continuously analyze the plan over a reasonable timeline and then make a final determination as to whether it should be adopted systemically. If the prototype is implemented systemically, the innovation team's work is completed. It is important to understand that once the innovation is finished, the team's work is finished. The team brought the innovation to a systemic implementation, and there is satisfaction in knowing that what you were charged to do, you did.

Education is not a business in the sense of having to constantly develop new products in order to compete on an almost daily basis. This differs from the business world, where product changes have to be made on an ongoing basis to meet consumer demands. Businesses are challenged to offer something new all the time. Every year, the major golf club companies offer new golf clubs and sell last year's "innovation" clubs at substantially reduced prices. Those companies are highly competitive and struggling to capture a limited market. Without constantly innovating and getting better, they won't survive.

Schools need that same mindset, too. The focus needs to be on continuously improving and achieving higher levels of success using new ideas if the old ones aren't working. But because schools work with students, and not simply consumers as in the business world, innovation must be done especially thoughtfully and carefully. To bring about the dramatic changes needed for some of the most pressing education problems, it is necessary to use an innovation framework and constantly review the results.

SUMMARY

The seven-step framework just described is intended to offer guidance for an innovation team and its coach as they implement an innovation culture in their district or school. While the steps are sequential, the innovation needs to be evaluated on an ongoing basis. The framework is intended to help a team work in a culture of dramatic change with a passionate belief that what it is doing will work. The team needs to be composed of members with diverse backgrounds who share a variety of perspectives on how complex problems can be solved. Short- and long-term evaluations are essential components of the innovation process, so the team must consistently assess data and what it learns from the prototypes to make adjustments to ensure a high-quality innovative product, practice, or program.

SOME INNOVATIONS CURRENTLY BEING USED IN EDUCATION

As mentioned earlier, the decentralized U.S. education system makes it almost impossible to move good innovative ideas to the thousands of school districts. It simply does not happen often enough. Unlike in business, when consumers clamor for good innovations such as the next generation of the iPhone, or in medicine, in which ongoing improvements become part of the training for all future medical practitioners, educators seem to be on their own in terms of finding innovative solutions to their most vexing problems.

This section presents some examples of promising innovative ideas in the field of education. It is important to emphasize that these ideas are in all likelihood not the result of an innovation process. Instead, they are examples of products, programs, and practices that offer the potential to improve teaching and learning. These innovative ideas may not have emanated from the seven-step framework, but they are intended to solve complex and/or persistent problems and used data or evidence to support a high potential to succeed. I offer these examples in the hopes that districts and schools may be able to use or replicate them.

It is also important to know that there are likely countless innovative ideas being used in schools across the country. What is needed is an effective communication system that enables educators to share them. That right there is an opportunity for someone to create an innovative idea that would help many educators struggling with similar issues.

Australia's Leadership Professional Development Initiative

In an effort to reduce transportation costs to the regional center for principals in remote areas and improve digital skills, the Northern Territory government partnered with the Association of Northern Territory School Education Leaders to offer its conference in an online format for teachers' professional development. It was felt that the online format would contain costs for the annual conference. The plan is now to alternate each year between using online and physical settings. Another innovative aspect of the conference was the decision to make it available worldwide in order to attract breadth and depth of papers and online discussion of school leadership. Debra Brydon, one of the conference coordinators, says that the "e-vent" attracted considerable international participation (personal communication, January 26, 2009).

The Northern Territory school leaders' innovative uses of technology reduced costs for the meeting and expanded participation worldwide using the Internet, and at the same time their organization gained exposure.

New Hampshire's Vision for High School Redesign

Trying to solve a problem using an innovative approach across an entire state presents a formidable challenge. New Hampshire's work to redesign high schools and improve student success through extended learning opportunities is a good example of an innovative solution to a statewide problem. Granted, New Hampshire is not a large state, but knowing the process it used and how it is implementing the innovations could inform a similar state initiative in other states, regardless of their size.

State officials in New Hampshire felt that too many students spent too much time in the classroom doing things that weren't relevant to their current or future prospects. The officials recognized that there was a need to improve high school students' preparation so that they graduate ready for college, work, citizenship, and life. In order to achieve the mission, they set three goals:

- Reduce the dropout rate and increase the compulsory school age.
- Improve the quality of data used to make sound educational decisions, and improve instruction.
- Implement a Follow the Child initiative.

New Hampshire's Follow the Child initiative supports a theory of action that students will do better in personal, social, physical, and academic domains only if their progress would be monitored over time in each domain. The process involves parents, educators, and the student working together to determine the student's learning plan. The plan is assessed using both formative and summative assessments, which are based on students demonstrating what they have learned and incorporate the principle of applied knowledge.

In addition, through a grant from the Nellie Mae Education Foundation, the state started a complementary initiative called Supporting Student Success Through Extended Learning Opportunities (SSS-ELO). This initiative was based on the premise that more students would successfully complete high school if they could earn course credits through learning activities that take place outside the traditional classroom and school day. To ensure innovation in designing new learning opportunities without diluting the required academic content, the credit-bearing courses must be jointly designed by participating students, teachers, and community partners. They must also result in rigorous demonstration of mastery of state standards and course competencies. Some of the learning activities include independent study under the supervision of outside mentors, internships and apprenticeships, community service, and service-learning activities; many involve a combination of outside learning with at least some classroom instruction.

These two initiatives were the result of identifying the problems of inadequate preparation for college or the workforce and a high dropout rate. The initiatives resulted in bold, new conceptual thinking about how to solve these problems. The state used data, collaboration, and a form of prototyping to implement the initiatives.

The rigor and quality of these programs are maintained through course competencies aligned with state standards and curriculum frameworks. New Hampshire was careful to ensure that the new initiatives were not perceived as an easy way for students to earn credits or for districts to reduce teaching staffs by sending students elsewhere for credits. Participating schools were encouraged to initially offer ELOs in social studies/civics/economics but also to develop at least one other content area.

New Hampshire's Follow the Child and Supporting Student Success Through Extended Learning Opportunities programs are based on the imperative that each student be given every opportunity to learn and attain knowledge and skills in a way that is personally meaningful to the student. Both initiatives are predicated on the premise that knowing the whole child deeply over time will lead to greater student engagement, more rigorous learning, 21st-century skills attainment, high school completion, and postsecondary retention at demonstrably higher levels. It is the personalization of learning around a student's interest that is the key. **(Paul Leather, director of the New Hampshire State Department of Education, Division of Adult Learning and Rehabilitation, personal communication, January 12, 2009)**

New Hampshire is partnering with other organizations and districts to develop performance-based competency assessments, which may be used for the ELOs but may also apply to traditionally delivered courses. They will create a policy framework for extended learning opportunities, offer professional development to teachers, and develop communication strategies for local, district, and statewide stakeholders to build public support to sustain the initiatives for a long time. It is the New Hampshire

Department of Education's belief that partnerships are important for developing and implementing innovative solutions to problems.

A pilot program that is conceptually similar to the prototype stage in the innovation framework I proposed earlier is being conducted at one high school each in four school districts. Three other schools are closely monitoring to see how they can also begin to implement ELOs for their students. The purpose of the pilot program is to analyze how the program is working. In particular, the pilot is focusing on understanding how ELOs can attract and reengage high-need students and what design features are required to assure teachers, administrators, and community members that ELOs can be as academically demanding as traditional coursework, if not more so.

Prototyping and evaluating are essential to effectively implementing innovations. Both the Follow the Student initiative and SSS-ELO are based on specific goals that can be evaluated for successful implementation. New Hampshire's work follows an innovation model and a different way of thinking about high school education.

Pacific Learning and South Pacific Press's Literacy Program

There has been considerable criticism directed toward the education textbook industry. Too often it sold products and programs that were not based on sufficient research, didn't incorporate effective teaching and learning strategies, and were not motivating for students. Yet there are bright spots. Pacific Learning and South Pacific Press took an innovative approach to developing a literacy product that targeted comprehension strategies starting with middle school grades for its first product releases. These grades were known to be the most challenging for schools trying to improve reading scores. (In the interest of full disclosure, I attended a Pacific Learning education advisory meeting to offer suggestions and my opinion of the product. I am not an employee of Pacific Learning, nor do I receive remuneration from the company for this reference. My suggestions are solely based on what I learned about the product and how it met the test of being a good example of an innovative product for schools.)

Pacific Learning and South Pacific Press were confronted with several challenges. They needed to develop a new product based on credible literacy research that would use technology interactively between teacher and students and improve comprehension through highly interesting text for students in the target age group. The two companies also needed to package the product to meet a range of needs, from schools with the most advanced technology to those without. The result was Comprehension Strategies Instruction (CSI).

We completed a comprehensive literature search evidencing the needs of middle school students for explicit comprehension instruction. The *Reading Next* report, released in 2006 and coauthored by Professor Catherine Snow of Harvard University, laid out a compelling challenge to educators, and we took up that challenge. We also incorporated into CSI scientific and other evidence from the National Reading Panel, Harvey and Goudvis, Guthrie and Nuthall, and Alton-Lee, among many others.

Creating learning materials from such a formidable and diverse evidence base is very challenging because students and teachers need materials that are both highly engaging and effective, and to add to the challenge we decided we must use the new technologies now available to schools and for which there is a much less established evidence base.

Along with coauthor Toni Hollingsworth of the United States, the team also strongly emphasized the learning community approach, with a focus on metacognition. We want students to not only learn the comprehension strategies but also learn about themselves as readers, their strengths and needs, to discuss the texts with their teachers and each other—to get feedback on their learning—and to be able to apply the learning from CSI to all of their reading across the content areas.

Evidencing our use of new digital technologies was more challenging. There is solid evidence for our use of audio texts, and we were fortunate to have leading audio-text author Meryl-Lynn Pluck of New Zealand on our team to develop the audio component. But when it came to digital texts for the whiteboard and data projector, the research is scarce. Nonetheless we found several studies that support the growth of learning communities in the classroom using digital technologies, and this encouraged us to continue down this line. Nuthall and Alton-Lee have shown that repeated exposure to new concepts over a short period of time give all students in diverse classrooms access to new knowledge and strategies, and this influenced our instructional design, too.

Most important, we had great interest from schools piloting the materials as they were developed, especially from Becky Crozier, a U.S. teacher working in New Zealand. Becky and her students encouraged us to include in CSI digital and picture glossaries and video snippets embedded in text to support students' background knowledge. This aligns very well with research evidence about effective practices for ESL students. **(Neale Pitches, lead CSI author, personal communication, January 7, 2009, on how the team went about the development process)**

Although CSI was originally developed for middle school students, it is now available for students in Grades 3–8. It clearly identifies the research that was used to develop the product, allowing federal funding for those who need to cite research in order to purchase it. CSI uses short passages of text, and students are expected to use reading, writing, and discussion to solve problems, conduct research, experiment, and learn specific content areas.

The program is offered for use with interactive whiteboard technology, CDs with a computer and LCD, or overhead transparencies. Obviously, the most innovative use of CSI is with an interactive whiteboard because of how it can effectively engage the entire class. Imagine teaching a particular text passage that discusses a river of lava to students who don't know what lava is or looks like. Using an interactive whiteboard, the teacher simply touches the text passage in order to show a brief video of a river of lava. The teacher can also use the interactive whiteboard to highlight word definitions, picture glossaries, and specific text when students don't understand them.

The CSI program is an example of a bold, new idea. It isn't the only innovative product available for literacy instruction, but it is a good example of an innovative offering from a company that develops education products.

Advanced Academics' Online Learning

Online learning is growing rapidly in K–12 education. Consider these facts reported by the International Association for K–12 Online Learning:

- K–12 online education is a $50 million market growing almost 30% annually.
- Forty-four states have supplemental or full-time online programs.
- Thirty-four states offer state-led programs to work with school districts to supplement their curricula.
- In January 2007, there were 173 virtual charter schools serving 92,235 students in 18 states.

Clearly, the growth of online learning has implications for public schools. It is a technological innovation that has led to significant changes in higher education and will likely lead to more public school partnerships with for-profit online education providers.

There needs to be greater accountability and measurement of student outcomes to determine student success. There needs to be a standards-based approach to online learning so that we are meeting the goals of the state education agency. We need to make sure that we understand the needs of the learner and that we are appropriately meeting the needs of different learner types in the ways they best learn the information. **(Jeffrey Elliott, president and CEO of Advanced Academics, personal communication, July 15, 2009, on what changes will be needed in the future to enhance online education programs)**

Advanced Academics is a leader in the field of online education and is partnering with schools and districts in approximately 30 states. It offers a customizable online program to meet the unique needs of its customers in

Grades 6–12. The company uses highly qualified teachers who work with a web-based learning management system. It is accredited by the Commission on International and Trans-Regional Accreditation and the North Central Association of Colleges and Schools. It also meets the standards of the National Collegiate Athletic Association. The following are some key points about the Advanced Academics program:

- Students receive support from certified instructors, and student achievement coordinators and have 24/7 support.
- Teachers have an average of more than 10 years' experience teaching in a traditional classroom, and all have at least a bachelor's degree in their subject area and are state certified.
- Each full-time student is paired with a student achievement coordinator who frequently monitors the student's progress.
- Parents can have access to and view their child's academic progress.
- Most students in the program can earn a high school diploma through their local school district.
- The curriculum consists of more than 90 courses that are available 24/7.
- The program offers alternatives to the traditional school environment, including for home-schooled students. The company is a provider for full-time online high schools in Minnesota, Oklahoma, Washington, Alaska, and California.

First, purchasing services from an online education provider is a natural evolution from buying textbooks from book publishers. At Advanced Academics we understand state funding laws and compliance in terms of student attendance and educational programs for various student populations. We have to be a trusted advisor to schools and knowledgeable about how online programs need to work in their districts and states. It is not enough to just provide curriculum and teaching, even of very high quality. We have to understand the rules we are operating under because it is a systemic administrative-based operation. **(Jeffrey Elliott, personal communication, July 15, 2009, on what Advanced Academics is learning about working with public schools)**

You have to be in today's environment. You have to be courageous because in many ways you are going to be fought and challenged by school boards and parents asking for more options for their students, with those same parents saying not only do we want something new but it needs to be proven and tested. You will also be challenged by the current school staff concerned about their future. The school leader needs to balance the needs of all the stakeholders, and that is not just a leadership issue but also a strategic planning issue. **(Andy Scantland, of Advanced Academics, personal communication, July 15, 2009, on the advice he would give to school leaders who are considering online education)**

Washoe Online Learning for the Future

In the Washoe County (Nevada) School District, the Washoe Online Learning for the Future (WOLF) program provides services to full- and part-time online students. While there is variation in the number of days students have to complete their courses, depending on the number of classes they are enrolled in, students generally have 60–90 calendar days to finish them. The program has three full-time education technology specialists, approximately 400 full-time students enrolled, and 200–600 part-time students enrolled at any time throughout the year.

Each full-time student and parent meets with a WOLF counselor prior to enrolling to determine whether the online alternative will be a good option for the student. The counselor has to agree that the student has a good chance to succeed in the program before the student is allowed to enroll.

Some of the WOLF curriculum includes various regular and Advanced Placement English, mathematics, science, foreign language, geography, and history classes as well as electives such as Career and Technical Skills, Journalism, Web Development, Personal Psychology, and Art Appreciation. The curriculum also includes remediation classes in math, English, and reading.

> Counselors see it as another tool. District leaders are concerned about home and private schools siphoning off district students, resulting in lost revenue. They see it as an option for retaining students in the district, helping provide additional classes for smaller schools, and helping them address the equity issue. **(Kathy Reynolds, education technology specialist, Washoe County School District, personal communication, July 23, 2009, on whether the online option is seen as an education innovation)**

Florida Virtual School

The Florida Virtual School is an entirely online statewide public school that is a partnership with the University of Central Florida. The virtual school plan is to determine what it will take to manage a diverse group of students. These students could be studying via computer anywhere in the world at their own pace at any time of day and requesting help with assignments by e-mail or other new communication technologies.

The Florida Virtual School is just one example of many online education opportunities being offered around the country. Online education will be transformational; over time it will radically change how schools operate. It offers opportunities heretofore not available to students in some very rural areas or in school districts that can't find teachers in hard-to-staff subjects such as physics, foreign language, and special education.

Only time will tell whether online education will be the breakthrough that many believe, but it is an innovation that is gaining acceptance on a much larger scale. Perhaps it will be like the laser in eye surgery and present the first real breakthrough in changing the amount of time students spend in school for classes.

Westminster School District's Elimination of Grade Levels

The Westminster (Colorado) School District has eliminated grade levels for elementary and middle school students in an attempt to reinvent itself while trying to improve test scores and dropout rates. Over time, Westminster intends to have 10 multiage levels rather than 12 grades, and students could be in different levels depending on the subject they are studying.

Nintendo Wii and DS as Instructional Tools

Nintendo, the game manufacturer that has developed the very popular Wii and DS gaming devices, is also providing gaming ideas that spawn innovation in education. Seventy teachers across the country are piloting a Wii music instruction program in their classrooms. The music teachers are commenting that using the Wii gives students access to the nearly 60 musical instruments that the gaming system mimics. Creative and effective use of technology combined with high-quality teaching is something that many critics of education have been suggesting for years. The opportunity to innovate using gaming technology may only be the tip of the iceberg.

In Japan, eighth-grade teachers at Otokoyama Higashi Junior High School use the Nintendo DS for spelling lessons. Students use the styluses to write English words on the touchscreens, and electronic voices tell them that the word is spelled correctly or offer words of encouragement if students get it wrong. One student was quoted as saying that worksheets were a pain and the DS makes learning activities more like a game. Many of Nintendo's software packages for the DS are actually learning resources and are easily adaptable to school activities.

I have to believe that technological innovation is at the core of what education is about, not on the margins or periphery. So the whole idea is moving to a customized learning environment that recognizes that students learn differently and at different paces. That can be accomplished now, whereas a decade ago it probably couldn't have. **(Former Florida Governor Jeb Bush, personal communication, July 20, 2009)**

The Broad Foundation's Harvard Laboratory

The Broad Foundation is contributing $6 million in grant funding for an education research and development laboratory at Harvard University, the purpose of which is to foster innovation and objective measurement of the effectiveness of programs in urban K–12 school districts. The program is starting in New York City, Chicago, and the District of Columbia. The lab will search for successful innovative strategies to narrow the achievement gap and ensure that students who have had the least success in public schools can produce dramatic results. Of particular interest is a comment from one of researchers, a Harvard economist, who notes that the new institute would be able to identify what works so that educators across the country could prioritize their spending (Hernandez, 2008).

The Offshore New Harbor Project

A good example of innovative thinking related to classroom instruction took place in the classroom of Shakira Petit, who teaches at the Promise Academy Charter School, in New York. Petit was a participant in the Offshore New Harbor project, which sent researchers to Antarctica for two months to learn more about global warming. Students were able to take part in weekly videoconferences that not only gave them an opportunity to learn content in the classroom but also let them experience what was actually happening while their teacher was in Antarctica (Matthews, 2008).

New York City's 24-Hour School

A pilot program at PS 5 is New York City's first 24-hour elementary school. Using the $200 laptop designed by Nicholas Negroponte, the school provides students with free laptops and Internet access. The online component will enable students, from their homes, to link to their classmates and teachers as well as access a vast array of relevant resources for their age levels.

Western Washington University

George "Pinky" Nelson, former shuttle astronaut and director of Project 2061, and now program director, professor, and graduate advisor for mathematics and science education at Western Washington University, has implemented a program using scientists to help teachers gain greater content knowledge.

> To me, innovation, especially in education, is doing what makes sense on a scale that makes it different. What we did that is innovative—that shouldn't be considered innovative because it's just common sense—is to spend a significant amount of time working as a group of scientists and content experts learning about teaching and learning. And we did a lot of that learning from our K–12 peers, teachers, so that we could be effective at helping them learn the content. It is an iterative process. **(George "Pinky" Nelson, personal communication, November 10, 2008)**

American Federation of Teachers Innovation Fund

Local school districts now have the opportunity to get funding from the American Federation of Teachers (AFT) Innovation Fund, which was created to provide seed money to "incubate promising ideas, promote proven programs, support risk-taking, and encourage shared responsibility for strengthening our public schools" (*AFT Announces Groundbreaking Fund*, 2008, para. 3). AFT is attempting to stimulate innovative reform ideas in schools in order to give students a world-class education, and it believes that efforts to improve public education and raise student achievement should focus on three areas:

- building the capacity of teachers to offer high-quality instruction
- recognizing that closing the achievement gap depends on more than just effective teaching
- fostering collaborative relationships among educators, their unions, management, parents, and communities

Massachusetts Institute of Technology

The Massachusetts Institute of Technology created a web site with free resources to improve science, technology, engineering, and mathematics (STEM) instruction for high school students. The site uses OpenCourseWare, which allows courses to be modified and redistributed for noncommercial purposes. The courseware includes syllabi, lecture notes, assignments, and exams. The project supports the increased emphasis on STEM education, which has been the focus of federal policymakers and professionals from those fields who seek to improve U.S. student performance in those subjects.

SUMMARY

It should be apparent by now that all sorts of innovation are taking place in education. Unfortunately, spreading the word about many of the promising innovations is a daunting challenge. Educators need to be given the proper context and conditions to generate truly innovative ideas. The innovators must be passionate about their challenge, willing to take risks, and supported by their leaders for taking those risks. The innovators also have to embrace the notion that their work must succeed, just as the NASA team had to succeed in bringing back the crew of Apollo 13. That Apollo mission could have ended in a disaster, but the passion, mindset, innovative thinking, and commitment of the recovery team prevented that outcome. And this is a good metaphor for how educators must address the most serious problems facing teachers and students today.

There isn't a cookbook for innovation work in schools. But there are ingredients that will lead to successful innovation initiatives. It takes effective team leadership, identifying the problem, an innovation framework such as the seven-step model offered in this chapter, experimental work to get it right, and evaluation that demonstrates it worked.

U.S. education received an opportunity to be innovative in 2009 by way of the American Recovery and Reinvestment Act. Secretary of Education Arne Duncan set aside $5 billion to improve school reform efforts by rewarding states that work on classroom innovation. That money is a substantial investment in education, but only time will tell whether it will result in real innovation and lead to improved results. For the funding to be successful, new products, programs, and practices will have to be created that unequivocally result in dramatic improvement on the problems they are addressing.

> There is no limit to what is possible in education when we provide the resources to tackle bold reforms. As never before, the Race to the Top Fund has created the framework for innovative partnerships between the federal government and states to make a real difference, strengthen our schools, improve teacher quality, and most important, better prepare our young people to compete in a global economy.
> **(Congresswoman Rosa DeLauro, personal communication, April 20, 2009)**

DISCUSSION ACTIVITY QUESTIONS

1. Identify the three most serious problems that you think need to be fixed in your school or district. Discuss why they are serious, how you ranked them as the top three, and what evidence/data you have to support your selections.

2. Hypothetically, select a diverse team of 10 people to work on one of the priorities you listed in Question 1. Why did you select these individuals?

3. Using one of the priorities you identified in Question 1 and the team you selected in Question 2, go through the innovation process framework in this chapter and informally practice each step.

4. Design a prototype of your innovative idea to fix the problem.

4

Final Thoughts and Conclusions

COMPLIANCE

This book is my attempt to connect three important concepts to improve schools that are not often aligned: compliance, leadership, and innovation. They comprise a tripod for school success. Often, compliance with federal laws is something that drives improvement work without much consideration of the fundamental purposes for the compliance provisions. One very significant example of a federal education law requiring compliance is No Child Left Behind (NCLB). It has resulted in improved student achievement in many American schools and considerable attention being given to teacher quality, data use for decision making, and the need to ensure that all students meet state proficiency standards. Interestingly, despite the substantial criticism of NCLB from educators, it appears they have done a better job of responding to and implementing the federal compliance requirements in it than many business leaders and corporate boards did to correct the egregious acts that resulted in Sarbanes-Oxley being passed by Congress. Clearly, education is improving and the focus on solving critical problems is becoming part of school improvement initiatives, whereas the corporate financial situation at the end of 2008 and into 2009 seemed to demonstrate that some business leaders didn't learn much from what happened in the "Enron" era.

Yet considerable energy has been devoted by many, both in and out of the education profession, to opposing the compliance provisions of NCLB despite almost universal agreement that the fundamental purposes of the law were laudable. How ironic that the general consensus on these purposes was good, yet many of the compliance provisions were not. But as noted earlier, despite that opposition, educators have worked to meet many of the challenging goals of NCLB. Compliance isn't "fun" work, and education still has a long way to go to meet the ultimate goals of the law, but the process is moving along and, with persistence, will result in needed improvements.

It is also worth noting that NCLB was not implemented by the U.S. Department of Education as well as it could have been. More commitment by the department to work with the traditional education community and more financial support, as promised by Congress and President George W. Bush, might have led to a better attitude on the part of the educators who had to make the law work. The fact that some professional organizations, such as the American Association of School Administrators, American Federation of Teachers, National Education Association, and national principals' organizations, were not actively engaged by the department to help implement NCLB resulted in a less-than-enthusiastic response from these organizations to find solutions to the vexing challenges of the law.

On the other hand, educators could have been more open to embracing the challenge of improving the education of students who were identified in the subgroups. Many years of unacceptable low achievement by low-income students resulted in a significant achievement gap between them and their more affluent peers. Granted, not all disadvantaged students, English language learners, and students with disabilities were going to make adequate yearly progress. Yet there was sufficient opportunity to work more diligently to benchmark gains with those students on state achievement tests that measured whether they were meeting state proficiency standards or, at the very least, demonstrating progress toward meeting them.

NCLB required those responsible for implementing it at the federal level to adopt a leadership style that would embrace followers with a more zealous commitment to comply with the law and not a fear of the law's sanctions. I don't mean that the sanctions weren't important, but from a leadership perspective, more effort to gain support from the stakeholders would likely have been a better way to get more enthusiastic support and compliance with the law's provisions.

Unfortunately, that style of leadership was not very evident. The tendency was to lead by using fear of failing to meet standards as the incentive for complying with the law's provisions. That leadership style was transactional, using carrots and sticks, when a more transformational approach might have led to more acceptance of the provisions that were the source of disagreement. Educators needed to believe that they could achieve results that were heretofore thought not possible to achieve. They needed to think like the Apollo 13 team that went through trial and error to find a solution that would bring the damaged spacecraft back to earth. Although, it is important to distinguish between the NASA mindset that failure was not an option and a systemic improvement mindset focused on innovation whereby failure is part of the learning process. The distinction is that NCLB is about systemic work and all those involved must believe that they can meet the most challenging goals to achieve success. The process of innovation will result in failures that are learning experiences contained within the process of systemic improvement work.

> I am a big supporter of having common or comparable standards and then having strict accountability. I am not a negative thinker about education. I think you can do much more with incentives than you can with punishment. NCLB was too much geared to punishment, top down. I favor bottom-up incentives to comply with the regulations. You get the incentives, and everybody is happy and moving forward. I believe NCLB served a good purpose and got everybody's attention. **(Former U.S. Secretary of Education Richard W. Riley, personal communication, May 20, 2009)**

From a leadership perspective, and with regard to compliance, several things would have been helpful for a more effective implementation of NCLB. Of course, I offer these thoughts with the advantage of hindsight, having observed how the law has been implemented since. The lessons learned are informative. First, the U.S. Department of Education could have done a better job of using the existing federal education infrastructure more effectively as a national process for explaining the provisions of NCLB. The department could have more effectively enlisted the work of comprehensive regional assistance centers, other technical assistance centers, and regional education laboratories to help states and their technical assistance intermediate service agencies implement the law. NCLB was too comprehensive and complex for state education agencies to process all of the requirements without considerable federal support in terms of both personnel and financial resources.

The department deserves credit for creating new roles for the comprehensive centers and adding five national content centers to help states comply with NCLB implementation. But much more was needed at the top leadership levels to gain support across the states for the centers' work. The focus of the department leadership was more on sanctions than solutions. More visible support for the centers, from senior members of the department visiting them and promoting their work from their bully pulpit, would have enhanced the centers' reputations in the states and, more important in terms of funding, in Congress. More funding from Congress was needed to really accomplish what NCLB required, particularly in struggling schools.

Second, cooperation from mainstay professional organizations such as the American Federation of Teachers, American Association of School Administrators, National Association of Elementary School Principals, National Association of Secondary School Principals, and National Education Association would have been incredibly helpful while NCLB was being implemented. Instead, these organizations were viewed by the administration as obstacles and were not encouraged to be at the table for discussions regarding successful implementation of the law. The membership of these organizations essentially comprises almost all education practitioners; involving them more would have been helpful while trying to gain acceptance of the most challenging compliance requirements that included serious sanctions. Many years of what might have been more support for overcoming the daunting compliance challenges of NCLB were simply lost. The reality of making federal education compliance work involves bringing all stakeholders to the table and working diligently to get a collaborative effort from them. You simply can't expect compliance in a decentralized federal system without the support of those who are expected to make it work.

Compliance with federal mandates is part of everyday life in American society, and sometimes compliance data can be mind boggling. One example relates to complying with federal income tax laws. In an opinion column in *The Wall Street Journal,* Nina Olson (2009) reported that "U.S. taxpayers and businesses spend about 7.6 billion hours a year complying with the filing requirements of the Internal Revenue Code" (para. 4). While this example may appear extreme, it would be quite informative to have such data on the amount of time a school system devotes to federal compliance and compare it to the amount of funding it received. The general consensus is that school districts receive about 7–9% of their total funding from federal sources. If one calculated the time and cost invested in compliance with federal laws, rules, and regulations, would it exceed the 9% total of federal revenue received? The issue is whether compliance is actually even worth the time and money when there is an option.

Interestingly, the financial support that the federal government provided in 2008 and 2009 for failing businesses has not been as well received as one would imagine. You would think that receiving billions of dollars from the federal government would be appreciated, particularly by businesses going bankrupt. Yet the businesses discovered that the federal "gift" doesn't come without some compliance provisions. And if a business discovers that is doesn't like those compliance provisions, it isn't always simple to change direction. One good example is Goldman Sachs. After only six months, Goldman Sachs decided it wanted to return the federal money it received in order to "extricate itself from heightened federal control" (Story, 2009, p. B1). But the government might not be willing to accept the returned funds so quickly and may conclude that federal compliance regulations on the financial industry are in the best interest of the American public. That thinking—about federal control over a private sector business—could lead to more compliance issues for school districts that receive federal funding. There is little evidence that the federal role in education is going to be less demanding with respect to meeting benchmarks for students who have traditionally not done well in school. Compliance with goals to narrow the achievement gap, improve teacher quality, build data systems that track students and teachers, improve struggling schools, and focus on 21st-century student preparation for college and the workforce appear to be a high priority in Congress that will not move off the radar.

The massive infusion of federal funding in the American Recovery and Reinvestment Act (ARRA) may come with even more compliance regulations in it than originally thought. As of this writing, school leaders were still sorting through the rules and regulations being released by the U.S. Department of Education:

> Stimulus funds have barely begun a slow trickle from the Education Department to school classrooms, yet state and local education advocates say the accountability measures attached to the money have already overtaken NCLB in accelerating reform and innovation, while placing an unprecedented, and somewhat uncomfortable, emphasis on spending transparency. (Sweeney, 2009, p. 1)

This characterization is not unlike some of the early criticisms of NCLB. In this instance, Congress has approved considerably more funding for education, yet the compliance provisions are already creating problems for school leaders because the expectation for bold, new reform and the reality of eliminating funding gaps as a result of reduced budgets is not easily reconciled. At a meeting with school leaders, Secretary of Education Arne Duncan said he did not want to see "tinkering around the edges" reforms. It seemed as though his presentation resulted in an unraveling of good intentions. Despite Congress appropriating the substantially increased funding to help education because of the declining economy, and more specifically giving Secretary Duncan $5 billion for education innovation to use at his discretion by awarding competitive proposals for this money, the school leaders at the meeting said that the funding was not going to accomplish what he was asking them to do.

Thus, the issue of compliance with federal laws, rules, and regulations is likely to become more challenging for school leaders and practitioners in the future. Compliance is no longer disconnected from the actual work of school leaders. In fact, it would appear that the benchmarks (particularly those related to teacher quality improvement, teacher preparation, high school student graduation tracking, and struggling school improvement) will be more clearly defined in the future. Federal compliance is beginning to impose serious accountability benchmarks for school leaders, who will have to undergo a transformation that puts more emphasis on systemic leadership by superintendents, building leadership by principals, and empowering teachers to take on a more substantive role in instructional leadership, benchmarking progress, and innovation activities.

> Supporting teachers doesn't mean deciding what professional development they need; it means enabling them to tell the principal what professional development they need based on their experiences with their students and then provide them with the resources to help their students succeed with accountability for outcomes. **(George "Pinky" Nelson, personal communication, November 11, 2008, on what might be different for the 21st-century principal)**

The notion that, because of compliance requirements for superintendents, principals, and teachers, the future leadership role needs to undergo a significant transformation is fraught with challenges, particularly the political ones dealing with governance and locus of control. Time and time again, school superintendents talk about how difficult it is to address compliance requirements with changing board of education agendas while maintaining focus on system improvement goals. Principals often discuss the critical need to review the most important tasks in their daily responsibilities in a standards-based environment by releasing them from some lower-priority responsibilities that could be accomplished by others. There needs to be a serious review of the expectations for principals and how they can effectively use building-level leadership strategies to help their staffs achieve high performance standards. This means getting teachers seriously involved in leadership roles, with both authority and support from their system and building leaders, as part of leadership teams. And it requires appropriate professional development for teachers on the process of leadership.

So while compliance requirements, particularly at the federal level, will become more challenging, accountability for meeting them will be determined by using data-driven information. Effective leadership strategies will be critically important to achieving success in this area. The need for a transition in the role of system leadership (superintendent) and building leadership (principal) and (teacher) is potentially diminished by organizational obstacles such as board of education governance that often focuses on noncompliance issues that divert the superintendent's attention from compliance requirements. Superintendents and principals need to accept that they will have to relinquish some of the authority they have traditionally had if education leadership is going to align with more contemporary

21st-century organizational thinking. If school leaders are going to be held accountable for rigorous curriculum standards and high student achievement, they need the latitude to focus on that work and not be distracted by a host of nonrelated issues. There is a plethora of literature describing many of the obstacles confronted by superintendents, principals, and teachers on a daily basis that distract them from the more important compliance tasks that require their attention. Stating the problem is much easier than solving it. But if there is a real desire to transform schools to embrace an organizational culture of high student achievement, it will require serious reflection on building a systemic team leadership model.

To help transform the model of education leadership, there is a critical need to accept the notion that teachers are part of the team. Education reformers need to support the needed changes in governance and leadership strategies for school leaders to realistically implement systemic and building leadership transformation. Superintendents and principals need to provide support, professional development, and the resources teachers will need to take on leadership roles. While there are examples of this leadership change is some schools, it needs to be universally accepted and embedded in the culture and leadership process in order to actually work.

LEADERSHIP

A good portion of the previous compliance discussion includes some of the transformational changes needed for education leadership to succeed in the 21st century. As I noted in the Preface of this book, it is difficult to separate the activities for compliance, leadership, and innovation. In *Achieving World Class Schools*, a book I coauthored with David Kroeze (2002), we use a genetic model as a metaphor for school improvement. Just as genetics is about a complex, living, dynamic human organism, school districts are complex, living, dynamic organizations. Both necessitate the simultaneous, seamless, integrated functions of numerous processes to function effectively. In human genetics, if an individual inherits "defective" genes, it will affect the overall functioning and condition of the body. Similarly, if a school district engages in multiple improvement activities (e.g., leadership, professional development, capacity building, curriculum development) that are not implemented effectively in conjunction with each other, the chances for systemic success are severely diminished. Therefore, systemic and building leaders must strategically plan and focus on key core organizational areas to ensure successful implementation.

Regardless of whether one agrees with the provisions of federal compliance, there is one simple fact that must be understood: almost all school districts must comply with federal laws such as NCLB as well as other federal rules and regulations. A rational case can be made that more effective leadership could achieve better results when complying with these requirements. That leadership must emanate from the president and members of Congress using their bully pulpit to gain public support for the fundamental principles of the federal laws, rules, and regulations they promulgate. District and school leaders must get their staffs to better understand the rationale for those laws, rules, and regulations and how they support the important principles that will lead to improved student achievement and fulfill the federal mission to educate all students. I am not calling for passive acceptance of those laws, but rather for more energy to be devoted to leading and implementing them and working within the system to get the needed changes.

The traditional model of school leadership needs to undergo change. The concept of school leaders getting advanced degrees in educational administration from colleges of education and then becoming school principals or superintendents has become archaic. More and more school leaders are emerging from nontraditional paths to lead schools with a very different mindset. Some of the leaders of more prominent large city school districts who have taken on their roles without previous experience as chief education system leaders are U.S. Secretary of Education Arne Duncan, formerly in Chicago; Joel Klein in New York; Michelle Rhee in Washington, DC; and Paul Vallas, formerly in Chicago and Philadelphia, currently in New Orleans. Former Colorado Governor Roy Romer became the superintendent of the Los Angeles Unified School District, and mayors are taking a greater interest in the leadership of their city schools. Secretary Duncan has even suggested that mayors of large cities take over their schools if student achievement is unsatisfactory. If that trend continues, and there is little evidence that it won't, the role of a system or building leader will focus more on results-driven leadership rather than on the much broader general concept of school administration. While I don't want to diminish the importance of being visible and working with constituents, many school leaders are evaluated based on their popularity and personalities rather than their success in leading schools to high achievement. It should be noted that school system leaders who report only to mayors have an advantage over the traditional school superintendent who is often confronted with trying to appease five or more board members who have different priorities.

These nontraditional system leaders all consistently talk about making improvements in their districts that are evaluated by using data-driven results. Their focus is on accountability that they can discuss using definitive metrics. Klein, Rhee, and Vallas have become the more prominently discussed school leaders in the media because they are taking on some of the most challenging education systems and taking risks to change the traditional models of schooling in their districts. Granted, each of them has the support of a mayor or governor and they don't get bogged down in school board politics in the same way that traditional school superintendents often do, but they still have to lead and gain acceptance from stakeholders for their agendas. It hasn't always been smooth sailing for them, but they are attempting to implement new leadership strategies that could become part of other school district leadership planning.

The administrative preparation programs for school leaders that often focus on courses such as school finance, school law, curriculum and instruction, and others must be modified. These programs need to place greater emphasis on school leadership as a behavioral science and help prepare future school leaders with a better understanding of what it takes to effectively lead people in diverse political environments. That doesn't necessarily mean eliminating all of the traditional courses, but rather recognizing that the role of the school leader has substantially changed since NCLB was passed. Today there is more transparency about achievement results in schools, more pressure to ensure that all students are learning and meeting state proficiency requirements, more of a need to understand and use digital technology as part of daily work, and more of a need to improve educator talent through higher-quality professional development and dealing in diverse political environments. School leaders need to be better prepared for these changing leadership roles.

There also needs to be a better partnership between the federal government and schools that are confronted with the most serious challenges. Just as the major companies considered too important to fail were given considerable federal support to overcome their problems, some school districts deserve a similar federal response to support their leaders. It is ironic that education is consistently mentioned by policymakers as critical to national security, yet it has never received the type of support that was given to the banks, insurance companies, and auto manufacturers when the financial crisis posed a serious threat to their continued existence. The focus for businesses wasn't on sanctions but instead on helping the leaders continue their work. Companies that the government identified as failing, such as Bank of America, General Motors, and Chrysler, received both substantial financial support to overcome their deficiencies and human capital support from experts to analyze what needed to be done to restore their companies to success. In fact, President Obama actually created a task force of experts to help the American automobile companies develop a very different business model in order to enable them to be competitive in the global economy.

For education, the federal government needs to consider comparable funding with a task force of experts to help school districts develop new operational models. That support should be provided first to the bottom 10% of American schools to help them improve. The government cannot suggest that these schools don't need large infusions of financial assistance and intense consulting support from proven experts to address their most critical problems while offering that type of support to private sector companies that should have been able to succeed using profitable business models. That support must come with a clear understanding that the schools must accept the mandated recommendations from the consultants, with specific accountability benchmarks, in order to continue receiving the federal support.

And as mentioned earlier, some of the instructional leadership responsibilities in schools need to be delegated to teachers who have the authority, responsibility, and professional development to fulfill their new leadership roles effectively. This delegation of responsibilities involves implementing a different leadership model in schools, a model that takes into account the need to empower everyone in the organization to meet rigorous accountability requirements. That means using the transformational leadership model to gain support for the leadership vision. The traditional education practice of a superintendent or principal singularly leading a school or district to meet those requirements is not how 21st-century organizations work. Teachers must take on some leadership roles and be accountable for their work.

School districts must offer meaningful professional development on what it means to be a leader and help teachers understand the role they will play in implementing accountability strategies and innovation planning for the system with their colleagues. Doing so will be very challenging, but it is critically important to think about running schools with a team-based mentality in the 21st century.

In addition to the instructional leadership role for teachers, I have suggested that they serve as innovation coaches/facilitators to help develop bold, new, and transformational ideas for their school improvement initiatives. These coaches will need leadership and innovation training. Innovation leaders need to be good communicators and have the ability to gain stakeholder support for their initiatives, which is not an easy assignment in school districts.

It won't be easy for superintendents and principals to delegate leadership responsibilities, especially when they are held accountable for them, and for teachers to actually take on leadership roles that require accountability. The concept will be new to the traditional school culture, but for the 21st-century school leadership model it will be essential. While I am not presenting specific suggestions regarding how to empower teachers to take on leadership roles, I would offer that it is best done through local school district collaboration between staff and management. This is much easier said than done, but it is critically important to the future success of schools.

School districts must commit the necessary resources to make innovation part of their culture for change and improvement. Chapter 3 provided substantial information on what an innovation process looks like, a suggested framework for a school innovation team, and ideas from two major design thinking companies. Leading for real innovation in education will require a very different leadership mindset and some tolerance for failure when new products, programs, and practices are developed and implemented. Tolerance for failure is not the same as acceptance of it. Rather, it is a willingness to learn from it and continue to pursue the ultimate innovation in order to find a solution to the problem.

An important fact for education leaders who accept federal funding that should not go unnoticed is how the federal government exerted enough pressure on General Motors to dismiss its CEO because the company accepted federal financial assistance and had unacceptable performance. The fact that the government can exert that type of pressure on a nonfederal organization because it is unhappy with its leadership and performance is unprecedented. It is clear that federal funding use now transcends both business and education with much more accountability than in past years. While NCLB contains sanctions for reconstituting a school district that consistently underperforms, the lesson from the federal government's role in replacing the CEO of GM may be that it is easier to just replace the current school leader to achieve the desired results. Metaphorically, losing sports teams usually replace the coach or manager, not the players.

Finally, the entire concept of school governance needs to be reviewed. While organizations such as the National School Boards Association may oppose the idea of changing the role of local boards of education, there is enough discussion about it to warrant more study and collaboration to see what, if any, changes can be made to give education leaders more authority to fulfill compliance mandates. There are simply too many situations in which education leaders are embroiled in personal agenda differences with school board members that distract from their ability to effectively lead their districts or buildings. I am not suggesting that local control be abolished, but more latitude must be given school leaders to do what is expected of them without being distracted by so many personal political agendas. As someone who served more than 22 years as a superintendent and assistant superintendent, I fully recognize the implications of that statement. I believe in local control of schools, but the 21st-century accountability requirements on superintendents, in particular, necessitate a serious discussion about how they can most effectively succeed in meeting them. It is an inescapable fact that nontraditional school leaders are generally reporting to mayors and not to locally elected boards.

The suggestion about changing local school board governance is controversial. But without an open, candid discussion involving national organization representatives for school boards and school administrators as a starting point, it will be too difficult for state legislatures to enact needed governance changes in order to improve schools. As noted earlier, Secretary Duncan has called for more mayors to take over school districts in urban areas where there has been little or no improvement in student achievement. Change in education comes slowly, and modifying governance from local control of schools will be even slower. The time to seriously begin that discussion is now, and it must include all stakeholders.

Research has supported the notion that, next to teachers, effective school leadership is the most important factor for improving schools.

The roles of superintendents, principals, and now teachers must change so that they can better align with how organizational leadership is implemented in the 21st century.

INNOVATION

Innovation is the one concept that could lead to the dramatic changes that might result in high-performing schools. It represents the possibility for transformational products, programs, and practices that are different from what is currently being used and successful in ways that have not been observed. The innovations can be simple or complex. In school districts, the likelihood is that innovations will be simple. Just as Bernard Sadow took two existing products, wheels and a suitcase, and transformed an entire luggage industry by combining those products, in the proper context and conditions, educators could create transformational innovations using what is already available but in different ways. What is needed is the context and conditions that allow educators to explore an innovation process that is similar to what IDEO and Doblin use. Not many school districts can afford the services of these consulting companies, but becoming familiar with their work and using their processes to stimulate innovative thinking led by teacher coaches who have had appropriate professional development in leadership and understand that innovation could be a significant step forward.

School districts, individually or collaboratively, need to train some of their teaching personnel to lead innovation teams. The innovation teams must use evidence to define the most serious problems and then build, implement, and evaluate prototype solutions over time. The innovative ideas must incorporate a mindset that ultimately the innovation will not result in failure. This thinking does not imply that the team will not experience some failures while going through the innovation process. It affirms that attempting bold, new ideas will likely result in not getting the anticipated results on the first attempt. The key is to learn from short-term failures, fix them, and not stop until the innovation has achieved its intended goal. Education leaders and stakeholders tend to be impatient, wanting rapid results and often not tolerating failure. In such an environment, it would be impossible to get the people working to find a solution to the problem to take risks. Not allowing them to take risks is a big mistake. Those risks may lead to the success that was the goal for the innovation work. Having a no-failure mindset—that is, believing that no outcome can be considered a failure—is about finding a solution to a problem that was identified for the innovation and learning from temporary setbacks while implementing solutions. Without a no-failure mindset, innovative thinking will not spawn bold, new ideas.

The federal government gave considerable support to the concept of innovation through ARRA, which includes $5 billion of discretionary funding for Secretary Duncan to offer a competitive grant program to stimulate innovation in education. The plan is to spend $4.35 billion on a Race to the Top Fund for states to compete on coming up with innovative ideas that support four assurances required by the Department of Education:

- college and career-ready standards and high-quality, valid, and reliable assessments for all students, including English language learners and students with disabilities
- pre-K to higher education data systems that meet the principles in the America Competes Act
- teacher effectiveness and equitable distribution of effective teachers
- intensive support and effective interventions for the lowest-performing schools

The remaining $650 million is for Invest in What Works and Innovation Fund for school districts and nonprofit organizations to submit proposals that demonstrate they can close the achievement gap and use innovative models of best practices.

Whether this $5 billion will actually result in dramatic improvements in education remains to be seen, but it is assuredly the most significant amount of money the federal government has ever put into a funding stream for innovation in education. The Invest in What Works and Innovation Fund for local school districts offers a truly unique opportunity for developing different approaches to solving the challenges of the four assurances that for many years have not resulted in much improvement in schools.

Educators need innovative new products, practices, and programs that transform their work with better results. Finding innovations that help all children learn should be the primary goal for educators in the 21st century. That doesn't mean the burden falls solely on their shoulders. There are numerous variables that are beyond the means of schools and districts to overcome. But there is potential for substantial improvement in what is going to become a more competitive environment for public schools. For example, one of the fastest growing delivery models is online education, and it has the potential to become a serious competitor to brick-and-mortar public schools. Public school leaders need to think innovatively and do more to incorporate the virtual model in their curriculum. Digital books, online learning, online discussions with students around the world, online field trips, ongoing formative assessment of student work using technology, and a host of other virtual activities and resources present possibilities for student success that cannot be ignored. Public education is going to be confronted with the challenge of becoming more efficient as taxpayers continue to resist spending more for education. Thus, the drive for innovation in business, to develop better products and practices while reducing costs, may very well become the model for innovation in public schooling.

I want to conclude with a brief overview of what Intel, a major technology company, says is the future for a 21st-century education infrastructure. First, there will be more interactivity between schools, parents, and students, including using Web 2.0 resources such as social networks, blogs, and wikis. Intel says that Web 2.0 is a shift from hearing and remembering to discovering and doing.

The company also says that gaming will be used more to improve student performance, skills, grades, and engagement. Earlier in this book, I described how the Nintendo DS and Wii are being used in classrooms. The promise of interactive gaming as a learning resource for students is a significant transformation from the traditional classroom use of print resources as primary instructional material.

Data-driven decision making will become even more sophisticated in the future. Intel says that using data will enable schools to replace large, bureaucratic structures and improve decision making.

The Intel model predicts that there will be more video and web conferencing because it provides new opportunities for collaboration without geographic boundaries. It is also more economical because it precludes the need to travel. The use of video and web conferencing is limited only by the imagination of those who use it.

Intel's predictions also touch on the future growth of networks and how they will incorporate parent notification systems, help develop more efficient transportation systems, and streamline student data to make it more useable for everyone within the school system.

In the Preface I mentioned my friend Jerry Citron, the attorney who said that I should suggest that those who are not serious about working to improve schools through compliance, leadership, and innovation should not read this book. Now that you have come to the end of the book, I sincerely hope that you took it seriously and have found the ideas from it thought provoking. I hope you will organize a discussion/study group, using the book to implement an innovation process in your school or district.

DISCUSSION ACTIVITY QUESTION

1. Now that you have finished reading about compliance, leadership, and innovation, what strategy can you develop to organize a study group to discuss next steps for your district or school? What are the most critical compliance issues? Who will be the leaders of this effort, and how will they engage the staff to implement solutions to the most critical problems? How will you develop an innovation plan and train staff to lead the process?

FINAL WORDS

Gina Burkhardt, CEO of Learning Point Associates

I am pleased to contribute to this book on compliance, leadership, and innovation because it offers a timely convergence of topics, to say the least. The book's message is important for anyone who is exploring and embracing new territories for reform in education. Understanding the triangulation of these three concepts may help clarify the opportunities and challenges ahead. And Paul is the right person to author such a book. As a superintendent in some very challenging school districts, Paul never settled for the status quo. He led the effort for his district and a consortium of 19 other school districts in Illinois to participate in the Third International Mathematics and Science Study when few believed it was possible for American students to be competitive with students from the highest-achieving countries. Paul and his consortium accepted the challenge, and their students emerged as first in the world. By taking this risk, the consortium changed how many districts viewed world competitiveness as a reality.

In this book, Paul provides sound examples, comments, and food for thought. The interviews he conducted—with policymakers to practitioners to business and community members—demonstrate the diversity of interest in and opinions on innovation. And while definitions differ, expected outcomes vary, and understanding of the innovation process is highly divergent, there is overwhelming agreement that now is the time and that education *has* to be the venue for innovation. To this mix, I dare to add a few of my own insights.

Over the past year, Learning Point Associates studied, watched, listened, and learned about how businesses integrate the conditions for innovation into their systems. Our biggest "aha" from all of this: innovation is both an art and a science. The science of innovation requires discipline—discipline that is not bound by typical rules and regulations. Innovation demands that its promoters act with intention and a commitment to structured practice. One cannot put a group of smart people in a room, say "Innovate," and expect great things to happen. Innovation is not a naturally occurring event, and no one person should be designated as chief innovator. The art of innovation demands that you train yourself to truly open your eyes and see things in very new and different ways. Innovation is, I believe, comparable to what those detectives on crime investigation television shows do every single night (ad nauseum?). They persist with their eyes wide open—watching, listening, asking questions—until they see the obvious and solve the crime. They do not, and we cannot, brainstorm our way to discovery. It is so clear that the more entrenched we are in a set of beliefs, practices, or processes, the harder it is to get past our expectations and see a new path forward.

Honestly, I despaired that innovative change would never take hold in our public education system. In education there are so many barriers to innovation. Governance structures, policies and procedures, lack of strong communication networks, contractual requirements for the workforce, lack of collegial time—the list goes on and on. Opportunities to create a discipline of innovation inside the system are dismal, the innovative practices happening are "by exception," and scale-up is rare. I began asking myself whether I would ever see real progress toward excellence. I did not see the will to break the status quo in a system steeped in tradition—a system often fighting hard to keep districts, schools, and state education agencies looking the same as they did decades ago.

I am no longer pessimistic. I am energized by the new wave of thinking and doing that has been taking hold of education this past year. I love the fact that really smart people from a variety of disciplines are taking deliberate action, forming conscious collaborations, and pushing the boundaries. The conversations are not about what we can't do and why we can't, but rather how to meet the challenges head on and conquer them.

The components of innovation are coming together and will rock the foundation of traditional education. Communication and social networks are inviting in more voices with new ideas and creative thinking. There are organizations and people that are systematically gathering this information and using it in very deliberate ways to engage in the practice of innovation. There are more people who understand that innovation is about common sense—about watching current practice and then finding simple and effective ways to infuse efficiencies. This means that we are getting better at making sense of and fixing common "pain points." For example, I just read about two college women who have a new and flourishing business making folding shoes. Their pain point (literally) was in their feet, caused by wearing high heels. Their solution: carry these fashionable and foldable shoes (that are not sneakers) in your purse, and slip them on when the pain becomes unbearable or the situation requires speed. This type of thinking and acting is infiltrating the education system from the classroom to the state departments. Hooray that it has even touched the federal government's glorious bureaucracy! The energy level is rising, collaborative structures are being crafted, permission is being granted, chatter is picking up, and the resources are available!

The good news is that these new approaches in education and the people talking about them understand the value of wisdom and research and development. These people get that you have to start with a sound knowledge base, try and test new ideas, develop tools and methods, and take risks—failing fast and often, and fixing what failed just as quickly. These people also know that technology can and will play a central role—not gratuitous technology, but the kind that takes its appropriate place in making a solution more effective.

The even better news is that there is funding and support for this new discipline of innovation. Those who continue to fight against the rising tide will not win and (rightfully) will be left behind. Those who engage in learning about the art and science of innovation will be invited to practice and to push progress. They will be held accountable for connecting wisdom, experience, risk, and research and development in targeted ways. They will learn from their own and others' successes and failures. And the result will be that the education system in the United States will return to a path of excellence.

Appendix A

Biographies of Contributors

Sir Michael Barber

Michael Barber is head of McKinsey's Global Education Practice and founder of the Education Delivery Institute in Washington, D.C., which advises governments in the United States on implementation of education reform. He works on major challenges of performance, organization, and reform in government and the public services, especially education, around the world. He is coauthor (with Mona Mourshed) of the widely read international benchmarking study *How the World's Best-Performing School Systems Come Out on Top* (McKinsey, 2007).

Prior to joining McKinsey, Sir Michael was (from 2001) chief adviser on delivery to British Prime Minister Tony Blair. As head of Prime Minister Blair's Delivery Unit, he was responsible for the oversight of implementation of the Prime Minister's priority programs in health, education, transport, policing, the criminal justice system, and asylum/immigration.

The approach to delivery that Sir Michael developed is widely seen as constructive and innovative and has been described by the International Monetary Fund as "the frontier" of performance management in government. His book about this experience, *Instruction to Deliver: Fighting to Transform Britain's Public Services* (2008), was described by the *Financial Times* as "one of the best books about British Government for many years."

From 1997 to 2001, Sir Michael was chief adviser to the secretary of state for education on school standards, and prior to joining government was a professor at the Institute of Education, University of London.

His other major publications include *The Learning Game: Arguments for an Education Revolution* (Indigo, 1997), *How To Do the Impossible: A Guide for Politicians With a Passion for Education* (University of London, 1997), and *The Virtue of Accountability: System Redesign, Inspection, and Incentives in the Era of Informed Professionalism* (Boston University, 2005).

Sir Michael's advice on public policy, especially as it relates to education, has been sought by governments in over 30 countries, including Australia, the United States, Russia, Estonia, Chile, and Malaysia, and by major international organizations including the Organisation for Economic Co-operation and Development, the World Bank, and the International Monetary Fund.

Matt Burke

Matt is a research associate for the Regional Education Laboratory Midwest at Learning Point Associates. His work involves the use of geographic information systems to display educational data in a geographic context. He has created data displays for state- and city-specific dropout summits throughout the Midwestern United States as well as state and local education agencies across the country. Matt continually strives to refine his skills with cartographic software, geoanalysis, and new methods for data representation. He is an experienced researcher with a strong ability to think critically and formulate innovative solutions to specific problems and research questions. He is a member of the American Educational Research Association and the Society for Neuroscience. He earned his master's degree in psychology from Michigan State University.

Gina Burkhardt

Gina is chief executive officer of Learning Point Associates, a nationally recognized nonprofit education research and consulting organization that delivers high-quality, client-focused evaluation, policy, research, and professional services. The work of Learning Point Associates focuses on expanded learning opportunities; district and school improvement, including services to state education agencies; educator effectiveness; and data analytics. Gina has led the organization through its transformation into a diversified consulting organization with a $35 million annual operating budget, a staff of 150, and four offices in three states. She is accountable to the Learning Point Associates Board of Directors for the integrity and continued success of the organization.

Gina's expertise includes leadership, organizational development and systems change, district and school improvement, and policy research. She joined the North Central Regional Educational Laboratory in 1997 and was named executive director in 1999. In 2003, under her vision and leadership, Learning Point Associates was created to build on the strength of the regional educational laboratory, with Gina as the chief executive officer.

A lifelong educator, Gina began her career as a middle school mathematics and science teacher in upstate New York. Since then, she has held positions in higher education, managed school reform projects at regional educational laboratories, and consulted nationally and internationally on education policy and practice as well as education systems design. She completed her doctoral coursework in educational psychology at the University of North Carolina at Chapel Hill. She has authored publications and has given presentations on creating 21st-century learning environments, using data to drive decision making, and meeting the demand for effective research and development in education. Gina holds several key professional appointments, which include serving as a board member for the Partnership for 21st Century Skills and for the Knowledge Alliance (formerly the National Education Knowledge Industry Association). She is a member of the Consortium on Chicago School Research at the University of Chicago and a member of the Board of Directors for Editorial Projects in Education, which publishes *Education Week.*

M. René Islas

M. René Islas is a vice president at B&D Consulting, a national full-service advisory firm. He leads the Firm's P–20 education practice, which provides B&D Consulting's public and private sector clients with comprehensive strategies to dramatically improve educational effectiveness. René has spent nearly a decade leading education reform through practical and policy work at the U.S. Department of Education and in multiple state and local school districts. He created B&D Consulting's provisionally patented school improvement process, which is currently being implemented in over a dozen of the lowest-performing schools across the United States.

Appendix B

List of Interviewees

Members of Congress

Congresswoman Judy Biggert

Congressman John Boehner

Congressman Michael Castle

Congresswoman Rosa DeLauro

Senator Judd Gregg

Former Speaker of the House Dennis Hastert

Congressman Rush Holt

Congressman Mark Kirk

Congressman Donald Manzullo

Congressman Howard "Buck" McKeon

Congressman George Miller

Former Congressman Mike Oxley

Congressman John Sarbanes

Other Interviews

Debra Brydon

Former Florida Governor Jeb Bush

Dan Domenech

Jeffrey Elliott

Jennifer Fisler

Gary Huggins

Robert Hughes

Jim Kohlmoos

Paul Leather

Chuck Morris

George "Pinky" Nelson

John Pipino

Neale Pitches

Kathy Reynolds

Former U.S. Secretary of Education Richard W. Riley

Andy Scantland

Sandy Speicher

Tim Waters

References

AFT announces groundbreaking fund to foster reform, support risk-taking, and share responsibility for strengthening public schools. (2008, September 11). Retrieved from http://www.aft.org/presscenter/releases/2008/091108a.htm

American Association of School Administrators. (2009). *Transforming our schools: National Superintendent of the Year forum 2008.* Arlington, VA: Author.

Antonakis, J., Cianciolo, A. T., & Sternberg, R. J. (2004). *The nature of leadership.* Thousand Oaks, CA: Sage.

Barber, M. (2008). *Instruction to deliver: Fighting to transform Britain's public services.* London: Methuen.

Barber, M., & Mourshed, M. (2007). *How the world's best-performing school systems come out on top.* London: McKinsey. Retrieved from http://www.mckinsey.com/App_Media/Reports/SSO/Worlds_School_Systems_Final.pdf

Bass, B. M. (1990). *Bass and Stogdill's handbook of leadership: Theory, research, and managerial application* (3rd ed.). New York: Free Press.

Behrstock, E., & Clifford, M. (2009). *Leading Gen Y teachers: Emerging strategies for school leaders* (TQ Research and Policy Brief). Washington, DC: National Comprehensive Center for Teacher Quality.

Bennis, W. (2007). The challenges of leadership in the modern world: Introduction to the special issue. *American Psychologist, 62,* 2–5.

Booker, C., Doerr, J., & Mitchell, T. (2008, August 31). Better education through innovation. *Los Angeles Times.* Retrieved from http://www.latimes.com/

Buhler, P. M. (2005). *The new workforce: Five sweeping trends that will shape your company's future.* New York: American Management Association.

Childress, S., Elmore, R. F., Grossman, A. S., & Johnson, S. M. (2007). *Managing school districts for high performance: Cases in public education leadership.* Cambridge, MA: Harvard Education Press.

Clinton, W. J. (1997, January). Remarks to the First in the World Consortium, Northbrook, IL.

Daft, R. L. (2008). *The leadership experience* (4th ed.). Mason, OH: Thompson-South Western.

Darling-Hammond, L., LaPointe, M., Meyerson, D., Orr, M. T., & Cohen, C. (2007). *Preparing school leaders for a changing world: Lessons from exemplary leadership development programs.* Stanford, CA: Stanford University, Stanford Educational Leadership Institute.

Dillon, S. (2009, March 8). U.S. to nation's schools: Spend fast, keep receipts. *The New York Times*, p. A14.

Economic Policy Institute. (2008). *A broader, bolder approach to education*. Washington, DC: Author.

Friedman, T. L. (2005). *The world is flat: A brief history of the twenty-first century*. New York: Farrar, Straus & Giroux.

Fullan, M. (2009). *The challenge of change: Start school improvement now!* (2nd ed.). Thousand Oaks, CA: Corwin.

Gelb, M., & Caldicott, S. M. (2007). *Innovate like Edison: The success system of America's greatest inventor*. New York: Dutton.

George, B. (with Sims, P.). (2007). *True north: Discover your authentic leadership*. San Francisco: Jossey-Bass.

Gladwell, M. (2002). *The tipping point: How little things can make a big difference*. New York, NY: Little, Brown.

Grint, K. (2005). *Leadership: Limits and possibilities*. Basingstoke, England: Palgrave Macmillan.

Hankin, H. (2005). *The new workforce: Five sweeping trends that will shape your company's future*. New York: AMACOM.

Harris Interactive. (2007). *Firefighters, scientists and teachers top list as "most prestigious occupations," according to latest Harris Poll*. Retrieved from http://www.harrisinteractive.com/harris_poll/index.asp?PID=793

Hart, K. (2009, February 9). A new arena for hard-core sports fans. *The Washington Post*, p. D1.

Hernandez, J. C. (2008, September 25). New effort aims to test theories of education. *The New York Times*, p. B6.

Hord, S. M., & Sommers, W. A. (2008*). Leading professional learning communities: Voices from research and practice*. Thousand Oaks, CA: Corwin.

Hughes, R., Ginnett, R., & Curphy, G. (2006). *Leadership: Enhancing the lessons of experience* (5th ed.). Boston: McGraw-Hill/Irwin.

Institute for a Competitive Workforce. (2007). *Leaders and laggards: A state-by-state report card on educational effectiveness*. Washington, DC: U.S. Chamber of Commerce.

Katzenbach, J. R., & Smith, D. K., (2006). *The wisdom of teams: Creating the high-performance organization*. New York: HarperBusiness.

Kelley, T. (with Littman, J.). (2005). *The ten faces of innovation: IDEO's strategies for beating the devil's advocate and driving creativity throughout your organization*. New York: Doubleday.

Kimmelman, P. L. (2006). *Implementing NCLB: Creating a knowledge framework to support school improvement*. Thousand Oaks, CA: Corwin.

Kimmelman, P. (2007, May 31). Time to foster innovation. *Philadelphia Inquirer*.

Kimmelman, P., & Kroeze, D. (2002). *Achieving world class schools: Mastering school improvement using a genetic model*. Norwood, MA: Christopher-Gordon.

King, N., Jr., & Stoll, J. (2009, March 30). Government forces out Wagoner at GM. *The Wall Street Journal*, p. 1.

Kirkpatrick, S. A., & Locke, E. A. (1991). Leadership: Do traits matter? *Executive, 5*, 48–60.

Kirsch, I., Braun, H., & Yamamoto, K. (2007). *America's perfect storm: Three forces changing our nation's future*. Princeton, NJ: Educational Testing Service.

KnowledgeWorks Foundation. (n.d.). *2020 forecast: Creating the future of learning.* Retrieved from http://www.kwfdn.org/about/

Kotter, J., & Cohen, D. S. (2002). *The heart of change: Real-life stories of how people change their organizations.* Boston: Harvard Business School Press.

Lafley, A. G., & Charan, R. (2008). *The game-changer: How you can drive revenue and profit growth with innovation.* New York: Crown Business.

Lander, G. P. (2004). *What is Sarbanes-Oxley?* New York: McGraw-Hill.

Leadership for student learning: Redefining the teacher as leader. (2001). Washington, DC: Institute for Educational Leadership.

Leading for change: New training opportunities for education's executives. (2009). New York: Wallace Foundation.

Lencioni, P. (2002). *The five dysfunctions of a team: A leadership fable.* San Francisco: Jossey-Bass.

Love, N. (2009). *Using data to improve learning for all: A collaborative inquiry approach.* Thousand Oaks, CA: Corwin.

Matthews, K. (2008, October 30). Live from Antarctica: Teacher talks climate with her U.S. class. *USA Today.* Retrieved from http://www.usatoday.com/

May, M. E. (2007). *The elegant solution: Toyota's formula for mastering innovation.* New York: Free Press.

McLean, B., & Elkind, P. (2003). *The smartest guys in the room.* New York: Penguin Books.

Munro, J. H. (2008). *Educational leadership.* New York: McGraw-Hill.

National Center on Education and the Economy. (2007). *Tough choices or tough times: The report of the new Commission on the Skills of the American Workforce.* San Francisco: Jossey-Bass.

National Commission on Excellence in Education. (1983). *A nation at risk: The imperative for educational reform.* Washington, DC: U.S. Department of Education.

National Comprehensive Center for Teacher Quality. (2007). *Key issue: Enhancing teacher leadership.* Washington, DC: Author.

Northouse, P. G. (2009). *Leadership: Theory and practice* (5th ed.). Thousand Oaks, CA: Sage.

Olson, L. (2007, December 5). Academy in N.Y.C. prepares principals for toughest jobs. *Education Week,* p. 8.

Olson, N. E. (2009, April 10). We still need a simpler tax code. *The Wall Street Journal.* Retrieved from http://online.wsj.com/

Our view on improving schools: New York offers blueprint for local education reform [Editorial]. (2007, December 3). *USA Today.* Retrieved from http://www.usatoday.com/

Parks, S. D. (2005). *Leadership can be taught.* Boston: Harvard Business School Press.

Prokesch, S. (2009, January). How GE teaches teams to lead change. *Harvard Business Review,* 1–2.

Reicher, S. D., Platow, M. J., & Haslam. S. A. (2007, August/September). The new psychology of leadership. *Scientific American Mind,* 22–29.

Rosenthal, S. A., Pittinsky, T. L., Purvin, D. M., & Montoya, R. M. (2007). *National leadership index 2007: A national study of confidence in leadership.* Cambridge, MA: Harvard University, John F. Kennedy School of Government Center for Public Leadership.

Sawchuk, S. (2008, January 25). Poll: Voters want schools to foster imagination, innovation. *Education Daily*, p. 3.

Senge, P. (2000). *Schools that learn: A fifth discipline fieldbook for educators, parents, and everyone who cares about education.* New York: Doubleday.

Softley, I. (Director). (2001). *K-PAX.* United States: Universal.

Special report: Innovation. (2008, June). *Inc.*, 87.

Stogdill, R. M. (1948). Personal factors associated with leadership: A survey of the literature. *Journal of Psychology, 25*, 35–71.

Stogdill, R. M. (1974). *Handbook of leadership: A survey of theory and research.* New York: Free Press.

Story, L. (2009, April 14). Goldman posts profit and plans share sale. *The New York Times*, p. B1.

Sweeney, J. (2009, May 4). Stakeholders: Stimulus accountability eclipses NCLB. *Education Daily*, p. 1.

Tuckman, B. (1965). Developmental sequences in small groups. *Psychological Bulletin, 63*, 384–399.

U.S. Department of Education. (2000). *Before it's too late: A report to the nation from the National Commission on Mathematics and Science Teaching for the 21st Century.* Washington, DC: Author.

U.S. Department of Education. (2006). *A test of leadership: Charting the future of U.S. higher education.* Washington, DC: Author.

U.S. education secretary to push for mayoral control of schools. (2009, April 8). *Education Week*, p. 5.

Wallis, C. (2006). How to bring our schools out of the 20th century. *Time*, 47–56.

Index

CORWIN
A SAGE Company

The Corwin logo—a raven striding across an open book—represents the union of courage and learning. Corwin is committed to improving education for all learners by publishing books and other professional development resources for those serving the field of PreK–12 education. By providing practical, hands-on materials, Corwin continues to carry out the promise of its motto: **"Helping Educators Do Their Work Better."**